The Crew's
Pocketbook

Tim Davison

Anita

WILEY ✦ NAUTICAL

This edition first published 2011
© 2011 John Wiley & Sons Ltd

Registered office
John Wiley & Sons Ltd, The Atrium, Southern Gate, Chichester, West
Sussex, PO19 8SQ, United Kingdom

For details of our global editorial offices, for customer services and for
information about how to apply for permission to reuse the copyright
material in this book please see our website at www.wiley.com.

The right of Tim Davison to be identified as the author of this work has
been asserted in accordance with the Copyright, Designs and Patents
Act 1988.

Wiley also publishes its books in a variety of electronic formats. Some
content that appears in print may not be available in electronic books.

Designations used by companies to distinguish their products are often
claimed as trademarks. All brand names and product names used in
this book are trade names, service marks, trademarks or registered
trademarks of their respective owners. The publisher is not associated
with any product or vendor mentioned in this book. This publication is
designed to provide accurate and authoritative information in regard to
the subject matter covered. It is sold on the understanding that the
publisher is not engaged in rendering professional services. If professional advice or other expert assistance is required, the services of a
competent professional should be sought.

The publisher and the author make no representations or warranties
with respect to the accuracy or completeness of the contents of this
work and specifically disclaim all warranties, including without
limitation warranties of fitness for a particular purpose. No warranty
may be created or extended by sales or promotional materials. The
advice and strategies contained herein may not be suitable for every
situation. This work is sold with the understanding that the publisher
is not engaged in rendering legal, accounting, or other professional
services. If professional assistance is required, the services of a
competent professional person should be sought. Neither the publisher
nor the author shall be liable for damages arising herefrom. The fact
that an organisation or Website is referred to in this work as a citation
and/or a potential source of further information does not mean that
the author or the publisher endorses the information the organisation
or Website may provide or recommendations it may make. Further,
readers should be aware that Internet Websites listed in this work may
have changed or disappeared between when this work was written and
when it is read.

Special thanks to Laser Performance, Northshore Yachts and
Arcona Yachts.

Illustrations: Greg Filip and Kara Thomas/PPL.

ISBN: 978-0-470-66529-9

A catalogue record for this book is available from the British Library.

Set in 8pt Humanist by Nigel Pell.
Printed in China by Toppan Leefung Printing Ltd.

CONTENTS

INTRODUCTION

If you are a new crew a yacht can seem a daunting place. There are ropes everywhere, the loo has a mind of its own and the ceiling tilts to where the walls should be. Meanwhile, you are probably feeling a bit queasy and are worrying about the latest strong wind warning.....

Don't worry! Everyone feels like this at first. The Crew's Pocketbook will give you the basic knowledge to work the boat, be safe, have fun.... and be asked back for more. I have used the correct terms throughout, e.g. halyard. Each term is printed in bold the first time it appears, and is defined in the Jargon-buster on pages 109-112.

With this book in your pocket I hope you will have as many happy hours afloat as I have.

If you have done a bit of crewing this book will serve as a useful aide memoire to the basics, and should teach you a few new skills. If you have mastered everything here you will be a welcome addition to any crew, and will be feted by skippers to help sail their beautiful yachts to wonderful destinations!

If you are a skipper you will realise that as soon as people step on board, they are effectively crewing. They will immediately be drawn into casting off, tying knots, hoisting sails, winching and even steering. It's impossible to go over everything in your briefing, and any knowledge they can gain beforehand is a blessing. This book was devised to be given to new crew to read before they arrive at the dock. If you are lucky they might even practise their knots by the fire and try coiling and throwing a rope in their garden! On passage they can refer to it again, consolidating the teaching you will inevitably be doing under way.

This book is dedicated to all the people I've been lucky enough to sail with over the years.

Tim Davison

PART 1: FIRST STEPS

WHAT TO BRING

So you've been invited to go sailing. Excellent! Like the rest of us you will inevitably get hooked and spend the rest of your life planning trips, buying gear and dreaming of sleek yachts.

Below is a list of things to take. Remember, space is limited on a yacht. Just take enough stuff so you have a change if you get wet, will be warm if the weather nosedives and cool if the sun shines. You can always wash your clothes in a marina. Pack your kit in a soft bag (NOT a suitcase) so the bag itself can be stowed. Keep everything in your cabin, don't strew things about the boat or you will lose them, particularly when she heels.

Make sure you understand the arrangement: is bedding provided, are there spare oilskins on the boat, is there a lifejacket for you? Are you expected to bring some food, and will there be a kitty to cover food, diesel and mooring fees? When and where will the trip finish, and what is the Plan B for horrid weather?

Sleeping bag
Sleeping bag liner
Pillowcase
Towel
Washing and shaving kit
Sunblock
Seasickness pills e.g. Stugeron
Wet wipes
Polythene bags
Torch
Batteries
Pen and notebook
Knife
A float for your keys (when you drop them overboard!)

Mobile phone and 12V charger
MP3 player (for night watches)
Camera
Book and games (if stormbound)
Present for the boat e.g. cake, booze

Shoes (2 pairs, one for afloat and one for ashore)
Wellies (non-slip soles)
Socks (aircraft socks dry quickly)

Trousers
Shorts
Underwear
Shirts
Sweaters
Neckwarmer
Sailing gloves
Woolly hat
Sunhat
Cap
Sunglasses
Oilskins
Mid-layers
Swimming costume
Consider goggles and snorkel (or are these provided?)

Passport
Insurance certificate
European Health Insurance Card (E111)
Driving licence
Money and credit cards
Rail or air tickets

Ready for anything:
cap inside hood,
lifejacket, oilskins,
gloves and wellies.

That's better!
Cap, sunglasses,
sunblock, shorts
and deck shoes.

HOMEWORK

The idea of this section is to give you a bit of homework so you arrive at the dock with some useful background knowledge.

Wouldn't it be more impressive if you knew how to tie some basic knots, could coil and throw a rope, and were able to name the parts of the boat? Here are some things you can work on at home, to get ahead of the game.

Round turn and two half hitches
Use: Attaching a rope to a ring or post.

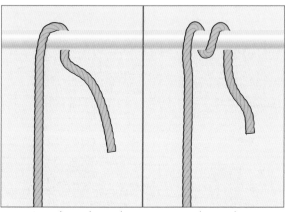

1. Pass the end round the object.

2. Take another complete turn.

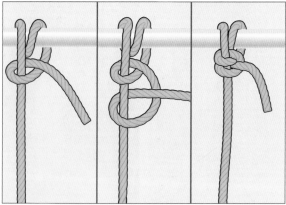

3. Take the end over the standing part, around it and back through to form a half hitch.

4. Repeat, to form a second half hitch.

5. Pull tight.

Clove hitch

Use: Attaching a rope to a ring or post.

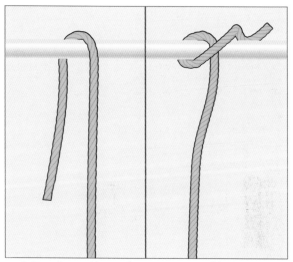

1. Pass the working end over the object...

2. ... and back over the standing part.

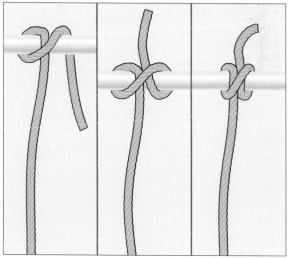

3. Pass the working end round the object...

4. ... and back through the loop.

5. Pull tight.

Figure of eight

Use: As a stopper knot. Stops the end of a rope being pulled through a hole.

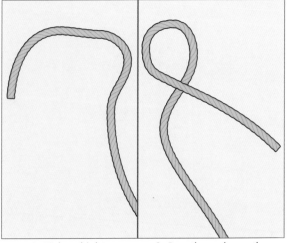

1. Make a bight.

2. Pass the end over the standing part to form a loop.

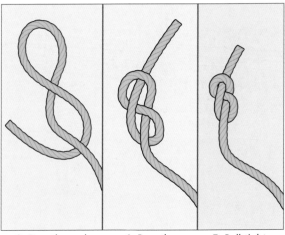

3. Pass the end under the standing part.

4. Pass the end through the top loop.

5. Pull tight.

Bowline

Use: Making a secure loop in a rope.

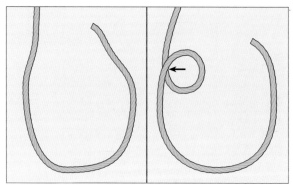

1. Form a bight of the required size.

2. Make a small loop.

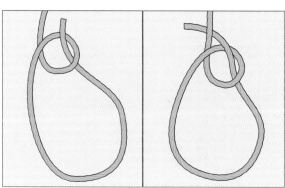

3. Pass the end up through the small loop...

4. ... under the standing part...

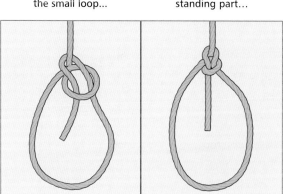

5. ... and down through the small loop.

6. Pull tight and check there is a long tail.

Cleating a rope

Use: Securing a rope temporarily.

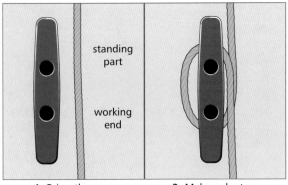

1. Bring the rope to the cleat.

2. Make a dry turn (once around).

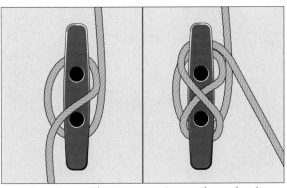

3. Begin to make a figure of eight...

4. ... and complete it.

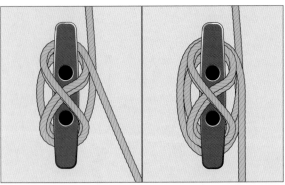

5. Make another figure of eight.

6. Make another dry turn.

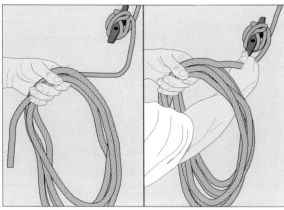

7. To finish off, coil the rope.

8. Put your hand through the coil.

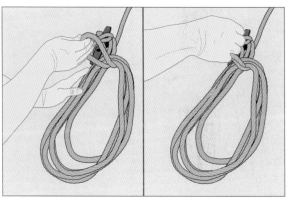

9. Pull back a loop.

10. Twist it twice.

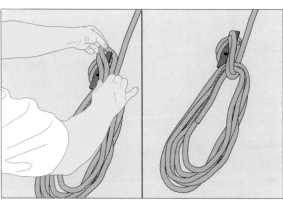

11. Hang the twisted loop over the cleat.

12. There you go – secure, neat and tidy.

Coiling a rope

The secret is to twist and coil the rope in a clockwise direction to stop it kinking. Finish with two or more turns and push the end through the loop.

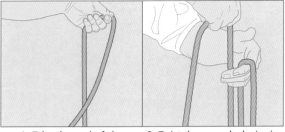

1. Take the end of the rope in your left hand.

2. Twist the rope clockwise in your right hand and transfer the rope to your left hand.

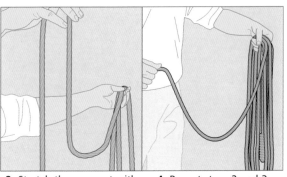

3. Stretch the rope out with your right hand.

4. Repeat steps 2 and 3 several times.

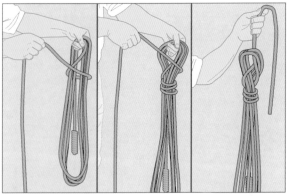

5. After you've coiled the rope take the working end around the coils.

6. Make several turns.

7. Put the working end through the loop and pull.

Throwing a rope

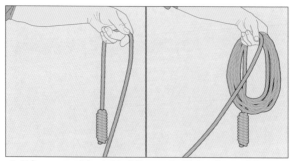

1. Take one end (weighted if necessary) in your left hand.

2. Make about eight small coils.

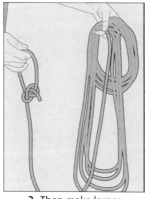

3. Then make larger coils with the rest of the rope. Make a small bowline in the end.

4. Separate the larger coils and put them in your left hand with the loop over your wrist. Take the small coils in your right hand.

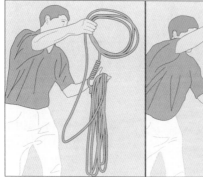

5. Throw the small coils.

6. Let them pull the large coils off your open left hand.

PARTS OF A YACHT

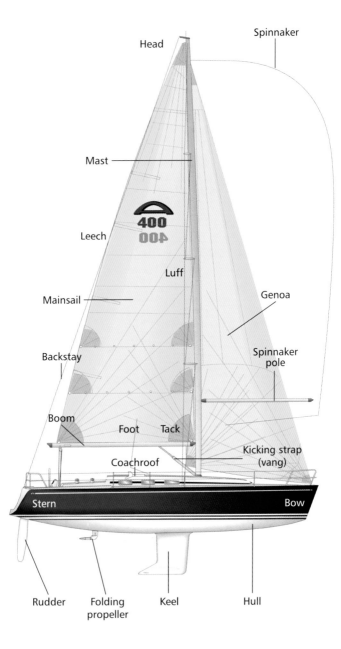

Head

Spinnaker

Mast

Leech

400
400

Luff

Genoa

Mainsail

Spinnaker
pole

Backstay

Boom

Foot   Tack

Kicking strap
(vang)

Coachroof

Stern   Bow

Rudder   Folding
             propeller

Keel   Hull

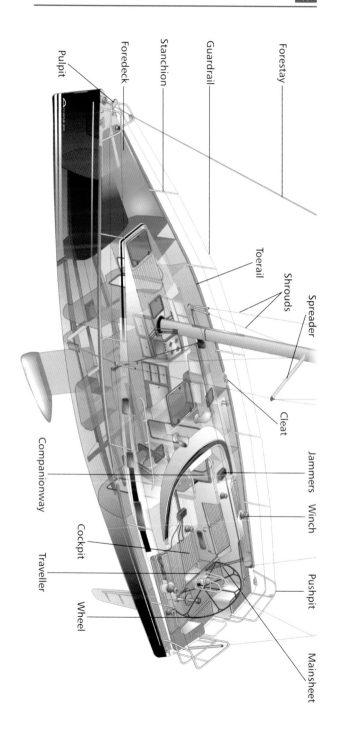

Pulpit

Foredeck

Stanchion

Guardrail

Forestay

Toerail

Shrouds

Spreader

Cleat

Companionway

Jammers

Winch

Cockpit

Traveller

Wheel

Pushpit

Mainsheet

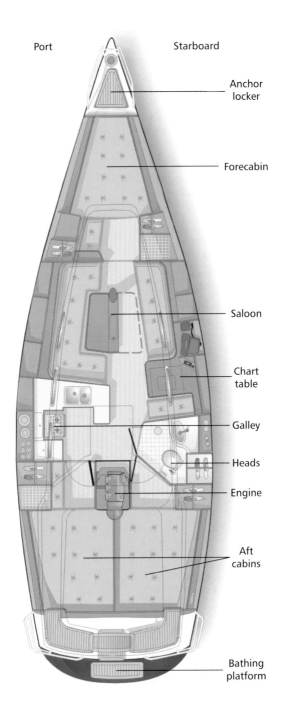

Port

Starboard

Anchor locker

Forecabin

Saloon

Chart table

Galley

Heads

Engine

Aft cabins

Bathing platform

GETTING ON AND OFF

If the boat is alongside a pontoon, it is relatively easy to get on and off.

Getting on with the boat alongside

Ask whether you should take off your shoes. Then pass your bag to someone already on board and walk to the shroud. Don't grab the guardrail.

1. Lean forward and grab the shroud, put one foot on the toerail and pull yourself up.

2. Transfer your second foot to the toerail.

3. Put one leg over the guardrail, onto the deck.

4. Repeat with the other leg.

If the boats are rafted alongside each other and you have to cross one or more yachts to get to your own, the etiquette is to ask permission to come aboard, then walk across the foredeck (not through their cockpit).

Getting off with the boat alongside

You will probably be asked to get off while taking
a line ashore.

1. Coil the rope and make sure
that it is led correctly.
When you are ashore, the line
should run straight from the cleat
on the boat to the cleat on the
dock, NOT over the guardrail.

2. Walk to the shroud
and hold it with
one hand.
The rope is in your
other hand.

3. As you approach the dock,
transfer one leg over the guardrail,
then the other. You are now
standing on the outside of the
guardrail, still holding the shroud.

4. If the boat has high
sides, squat down so
you don't have so far
to step.

5. As the boat slides alongside, STEP onto the dock. Don't jump! If the boat is too far away, the skipper will come round again.

6. As soon as you land, take a turn around a cleat or bollard so you can control the boat. Never stand there holding the rope straight from the yacht – it's heavier than you! Surge the rope until the boat comes to a standstill. Then pull the boat alongside.

7. Finally, secure the rope to a cleat.

Getting on and off when the boat is moored stern-to

There will usually be a plank rigged up and it's just a question of teetering along it. This will be made easier if someone pulls on the mooring rope to bring the boat closer. If you feel unsure, ask for the bow line or anchor line to be eased and the boat pulled in. Better that than a damp arrival!

Getting on from the dinghy

Often you will board at the stern of the yacht. Another crewperson will pull the dinghy tightly to the yacht and you can then step aboard. Climb up at the shrouds if boarding from alongside.

Getting into the dinghy

Again, make sure someone is holding the dinghy tightly to the yacht. Step into the middle of the dinghy or you may capsize it. Sit down immediately to aid stability.

THE SKIPPER'S BRIEFING

Before you set off the skipper will brief the crew.

Where everything is

He will go through the boat, pointing out where everything is kept. You may like to use the space below to make notes of where important items are stored.

Item	Location

Safety equipment

He will also point out all the safety equipment such as fire extinguishers, jackstays, lifejackets, lifelines, liferaft, dan buoy, throwing line, retrieval line, rescue sling, flares and tools.

Flares

Flares have a variety of mechanisms and uses. Your skipper will explain how and when they should be used. Wear gloves if possible. Two common mechanisms are 'twist and strike' and 'pin and push'. Always read the instructions.

1. Twist the end.

2. Strike the base firmly.

1. The arrows indicate which way is up.

2. Take off the caps from both ends.

3. Remove the pin.

4. Push lever firmly upwards.

Personal kit

The skipper will issue you with a lifejacket and help you adjust it. Ask someone to open it up and make sure the gas cylinder is screwed in properly. He will tell you where and when to clip on your lifeline and demonstrate how to move about the boat safely.

Now is the time to try on any waterproof clothing you are borrowing and find out where they should be hung when wet.

Operating the toilet

It's vital to know how the toilet (heads) works! If you are lucky, it will simply be a question of pulling a lever one way and pumping water through, then pushing it the other way and pumping the bowl dry. But sometimes the skipper likes the seacocks shut after use (which closes off the pipes leading through the hull). You should NEVER put tampons, sanitary towels or anything inorganic down the loo, and on some boats you are asked to put the toilet paper in a bag. The pipes are narrow, and it is all too easy to block them! If a septic tank is fitted, waste should be stored in this in harbour and pumped when offshore.

1. The machine!

2. Switch to flush.

3. Pump water in.

4. Switch back then pump dry.

Using gas

Gas is dangerous on a boat. Always turn off the tap after using the stove, and sometimes you will be asked to turn off the tap at the cylinder as well.

1. Unscrew the tap at the cylinder.

2. Open the valve near the cooker.

3. Press in the knob.

4. Light the gas and keep the knob pressed in for 5-10 seconds until the safety cut-out has heated up.

In a marina you can probably use as much electricity, gas, fuel and water as you like, but once you have left the dock remember that these are finite.

The VHF radio

This is your link to the outside world. At the briefing the skipper will show you how to turn it on, adjust the squelch, and send a Mayday call for help. See p83 to learn how to send a Mayday and for general VHF use.

What you can damage

- The guardrails are surprisingly weak. Push off against the toerail rather than the guardrails.
- Don't hold onto the wheel for support!
- Don't grab aerials when climbing aboard, especially over the stern.
- If you're using an electric winch, look at the thing it's pulling, not at the winch or button. The winch has enormous power and not much feel, so you need to see what it is doing.

What can damage you

- The boom is very hard and can swing across fast. Always duck when the boom is in motion, particularly when gybing.
- It is usually safe to hold onto wires, but not to ropes. The reason they are made of rope is that they are designed to move!
- Always put a rope round a winch before releasing it from a cleat or jammer. There could be a considerable load on it, and you will need the friction of the turns round the winch to prevent it burning through your fingers.
- You will usually need a winch to pull in a rope under strain.
- Be careful pulling up the anchor, or you may damage your back.
- Watch your toes and fingers if using a windlass to raise or lower the anchor. Wear gloves and shoes.

Seasickness

Tell the skipper if you are prone to seasickness. You can either do this at the briefing, or afterwards if you are shy. He will recommend a remedy and show you how to be sick safely (don't hang out over the side – you may follow your breakfast overboard!). Take seasickness remedies well in advance. Some people find pressure point wristbands (e.g. Seabands) effective.

Most people are best on deck, looking at the horizon. If you need to go below, get horizontal as soon as you can.

If you are feeling sick on passage, tell the skipper who will make sure you are safe. If the worst comes to the worst, remain seated and be sick into a bucket.

The Plan

At the briefing the skipper will give you the overall plan for the trip, and show how he has split it into smaller 'chunks'. For each, there will be a fallback plan in case things go wrong or the weather is atrocious. He will probably enter the trip on the chartplotter using a series of waypoints (see later) so you can see the boat moving from one 'X' to another as you sail.

Weather

He will also brief you on the expected weather for the trip. The data can be obtained from the harbourmaster, the internet or the onboard Navtex, or preferably from all three. But don't forget to look out of the hatch, the Mark One Eyeball gives the best short term forecast!

PART 2:
UNDER POWER

THE ENGINE

Starting the engine

The engine is your secondary means of propulsion. You will be shown how to turn on the engine, put it into ahead, neutral and astern, and turn it off.

1. Push in the clutch then push the accelerator forward.

2. Start the engine.

3. Pull the lever into neutral – the clutch button will click out.

4. Push the lever forward and the boat will power ahead.

Stopping the engine

1. Put the gear lever in neutral.
2. Pull out the stop lever or press the stop button.
3. When the alarm beeps, turn the key to off.
4. Push in the stop lever if necessary.

When sailing, the gear lever is usually in reverse to stop the propeller spinning.

Docking and casting off

A boat is usually moored to a marina pontoon or quayside by a bow and stern line and two springs.

The bow and stern lines hold the boat in to the dock, but don't stop it moving fore-and-aft. The springs stop the boat moving forwards and backwards (fore and aft) but don't hold the boat in!

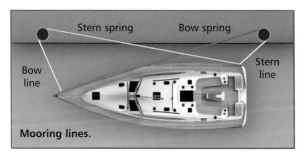

Mooring lines.

Casting off

If there is wind or tide acting on the boat, one or more of the ropes will be slack. These will be released first.

The skipper will probably now ask you to take charge of one line and double it up as a slip line. Then, as the boat heads out, you can either release one end and retrieve the line, or flip it off the cleat on the dock and pull the doubled line aboard. The key thing is not to get the rope round the propeller!

Using a slip line:

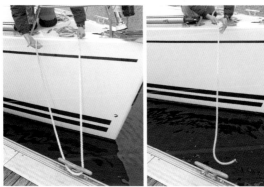

1. Rig the line like this.   2. On the command, release one end and retrieve the line.

Once away, coil the rope and stow it. Then take off the fenders and stow them too.

Springing off

If the wind is strong and pushing the boat onto the dock, you may have to spring her off. You can use either a bow or a stern spring.

1. Pad the bow with lots of fenders.

2. Rig the bow spring as a slip rope.

3. The boat is driven forward and the stern kicks out.

4. Retrieve the rope as the boat is reversed out.

Your job will be to hold one end of the slip line, with a turn or two on the cleat. When the boat is backing out, release this end of the line and retrieve from the other end.

Docking

You will be given one line to take ashore. Get ready as described on page 20.

As the boat arrives at the dock, step ashore and get a turn round a cleat, bollard or tree. Hold the boat, then pull her in. The easiest way to do this is to take some tension around the cleat, then pull sideways on the line, between the cleat and the boat. (You can get a lot of tension like this.) Pull the slack you have gained 'past' the cleat, and repeat. When the skipper is satisfied, cleat off the rope and go on to the next line you are given, which will probably be the spring.

1. Have the central line ready.

2. Step off.

3. Secure it to a cleat. The boat is now tethered.

4. Take the bow line.

5. Secure it.

6. Take the stern line.

7. Secure it.

8. Pull sideways on a rope to move a heavy yacht.

Steering

When you're on the helm your jobs are to keep on course, avoid hitting anything and prevent the boat running aground. If you are unsure, always call the skipper. He will prefer that to an expensive collision! Make sure you can read the depth meter and know the depth at which the boat will hit the bottom. Often an alarm is set, to warn you you're in shallow water. For example, my boat is 2.1 metres deep and grounds when the depth reads 2.1 metres, and the alarm sounds at 3.5 metres. (Some skippers prefer to have the meter show depth under the keel, so their boat grounds when the depth shows 0.)

Keep an eye on the depth readout.

1. It's just like a car.
Note the marker to show the 'straight ahead' position.

2. If you want the boat to go backwards, it's easier if you steer facing aft. Now it's like steering a car once again.

Keeping on course

If there is a suitable object ahead, you will be asked to steer for it ('head towards the smallest island'). Look straight down the centreline of the boat and steer for the object. If you want to sit off the centreline, you need to align the bow to one side of the object. (Technically, this is called parallax.) You will soon get the hang of this.

If there is no suitable object, or you are out at sea, you will be given a compass course ('steer 280'). The diagrams show how a compass works, but essentially the compass card is 'fixed' (it always points north) and you are 'steering the lubber line across it'. It's hard work looking at the compass all the time, and it may even make you feel queasy. Instead, get on course and then try to find something straight ahead – it might even be a distinctive cloud - and steer for it. The cloud will of course move, so every few minutes you need to choose a new target.

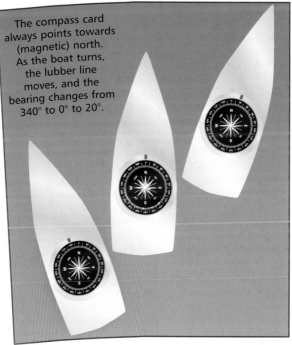

The compass card always points towards (magnetic) north. As the boat turns, the lubber line moves, and the bearing changes from 340° to 0° to 20°.

The other thing to watch is the sails. If the sails are flapping, you are either off-course or the wind has changed! Check the compass, and if you are still on course ask for the sheets to be adjusted.

Note that you can only steer if there is a flow of water across the rudder, i.e. you need some speed!

If the boat has a tiller, experiment with pushing
you and pulling it towards you. You push the ti
opposite direction to where you want to go (se

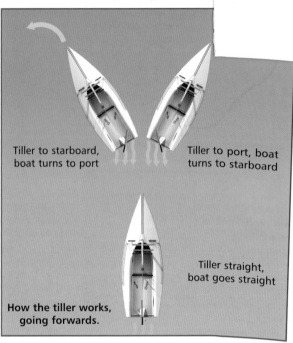

Tiller to starboard,
boat turns to port

Tiller to port, boat
turns to starboard

Tiller straight,
boat goes straight

**How the tiller works,
going forwards.**

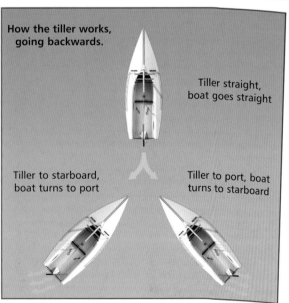

**How the tiller works,
going backwards.**

Tiller straight,
boat goes straight

Tiller to starboard,
boat turns to port

Tiller to port, boat
turns to starboard

Steering backwards with a tiller is tricky – begin by holding the tiller centrally so it doesn't swing hard to one side and always keep a firm grip on it. Then push the tiller towards the direction you want the bow to turn (see diagram). Steering with a wheel is easy – it's just like steering a car! If you want to steer astern, I suggest you move in front of the wheel and face aft, then once again steering is straightforward.

Many boats have an autohelm and this can be useful on long legs. Get the skipper to show you how to switch it on and off and adjust the course. Have a practice, because if something comes up unexpectedly you will need to switch off the autohelm quickly and steer manually out of danger.

RULES OF THE ROAD

Basic rules under power

If you think a collision is possible, call the skipper early so you have time to avoid the problem.

See also the section on lights and shapes on page 99.

If you are going to collide with another vessel head-on, both should turn right (and pass down each other's port side). At night, you will see the other boat's red and green lights approaching. After turning right, you should just see each other's red light.

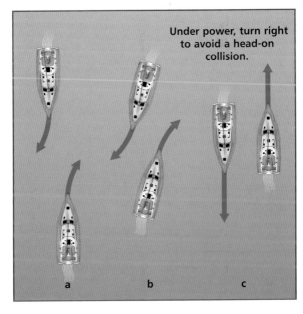

Under power, turn right to avoid a head-on collision.

a   b   c

If you are crossing another vessel you first need to check whether a collision will happen if you continue on your course. Sit still and line up the other boat's stern with something on your own boat, such as a stanchion.
If this bearing doesn't change, you are on a collision course. Now is probably the time to call the skipper! The boat with the other on its starboard side should keep clear, usually by steering to pass behind the other boat. This is rather like giving way to traffic from the right at a roundabout (in the UK!). At night, if you see the red light of the crossing boat you know to keep clear. He will see your green light and know to keep straight on, unless a collision is imminent.

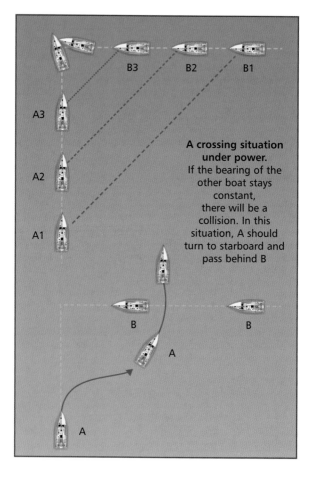

A crossing situation under power.
If the bearing of the other boat stays constant, there will be a collision. In this situation, A should turn to starboard and pass behind B

If you are overtaking another vessel you must keep clear, but you can overtake on either side. At night you will see the other boat's white stern light, then her red or green as you pass her.

If you are giving way, make a reasonably large alteration of course so the other helm can see you have made a change. At night, this means altering so they see different lights on your boat.

If you are motoring down a channel you will normally keep to starboard.

You will normally keep just outside a shipping channel, because large ships have no room for manoeuvre. This may involve passing navigation buoys on the 'wrong' side.

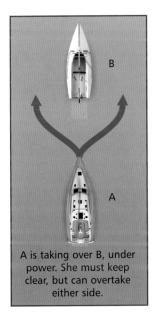

A is taking over B, under power. She must keep clear, but can overtake either side.

Navigating with a chartplotter

To begin with I suggest you steer towards an object or use the compass. But as you become more competent, you will no doubt want to use the magic box sitting in front of you, if one is fitted.

A chartplotter is loaded with charts of your area. You can pan out to see the whole trip and zoom in to see detail. Make sure you understand how shallows are shown (they may be shown by different colours from the ones on the paper chart).

The skipper will have put in one or more crosses (waypoints), and the machine draws a line from one to another to define the trip. These lines are the courses you are going to follow, and should not cross any shallows!

As you set off, a picture of a small boat begins to move across the chart. If you are going the right way, the boat will follow the line to the first waypoint. If not, you will see the little boat draw away from the line, and will know to turn a bit so the real boat gets back on course. At all times the chartplotter gives your range and bearing to the next waypoint (BTW), so you can see how to steer. The problem is that the boat won't necessarily go where you point it, because it will drift sideways in the wind and tide. Helpfully, the machine also gives the course the boat is actually achieving, the Course Over the Ground or COG, and your objective is to make the COG the same as the BTW.

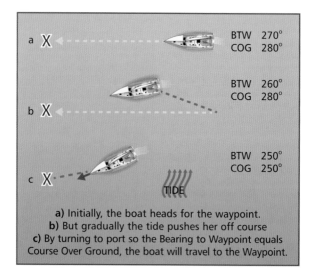

BTW 270°
COG 280°

BTW 260°
COG 280°

BTW 250°
COG 250°

a) Initially, the boat heads for the waypoint.
b) But gradually the tide pushes her off course
c) By turning to port so the Bearing to Waypoint equals
Course Over Ground, the boat will travel to the Waypoint.

Another useful aid is the Cross Track Error (XTE). When the
machine is activated, it 'draws' an imaginary line from
your position to the next waypoint, and as you progress it
tells you how far off this line (the rhumb line) you are.
It also tells you which way to turn to lessen the cross
track error. Turn gently in the direction indicated until
the boat goes parallel to the rhumb line or, if you have
gone a long way off course, reduce the Cross Track Error
at a sensible rate.

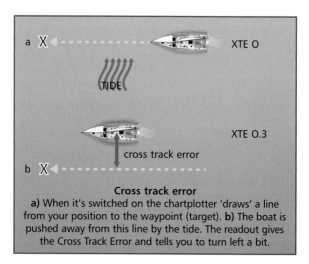

XTE 0

XTE 0.3

cross track error

Cross track error
a) When it's switched on the chartplotter 'draws' a line
from your position to the waypoint (target). **b)** The boat is
pushed away from this line by the tide. The readout gives
the Cross Track Error and tells you to turn left a bit.

When the boat reaches the waypoint an alarm should
sound, and the machine may automatically begin navigating
to the next waypoint.

Although it's possible to interface the chartplotter with the autopilot and have them steer the boat automatically, I don't recommend this. Better to have a human involved, keeping the boat safe.

I do recommend looking at the course on a paper chart before you begin your stint on the helm. In doing this you can understand the whole trip and see the detail. It is also a good idea to mark your position with a cross on the paper chart every hour (say) to check progress and also to have a fall-back position if the machine fails! The skipper will show you how to transfer your latitude and longitude from the chartplotter to the paper chart, and how to update the logbook that records the voyage.

Motoring at night

Let's assume you have been on watch in the daytime and are now turning in to your bunk but will be on watch again in a few hours, in darkness.

Before you go to sleep it's a good idea to organise your gear so you can get dressed again quickly and get on deck before you feel too queasy. Have your boots and oilskins ready, with your lifejacket and harness adjusted to fit. If your oilskin jacket has toggles, you can have your lifejacket permanently fitted to them. Have gloves, a torch and a woolly hat handy too – it can be cold at night. In daylight, note where the strong points are for clipping on.

Set an alarm or ask the current watch to wake you ten minutes before you are due on deck. It will be a major black mark if you are late on deck. Then have a good sleep.

Sleeping

Boots and trousers ready to be stepped into.

A leecloth will hold you into your bunk.

Hopefully they will wake you with a cup of tea! Go to the loo, then get dressed fully before you stick your head out of the hatch – a rogue wave always seems to hit you just as you appear! Stand on the companion steps and clip on before you go outside – you will probably still be half asleep and you want to be safe as you emerge.

If you're in luck, someone will wake you with a cup of tea.

Ask the helm what has been happening, if there are any possible collisions in the offing, what the course is and how the boat is going. When you're ready, take over. The previous helm will probably watch you for a few minutes to see that you have the right idea, then they will go below for some well-earned shuteye.

You must always be clipped on at night. Never leave the cockpit unless someone is watching you. Keep a sharp lookout, in all directions. If you see the lights of another boat approaching, discuss it with your companion or call the skipper. Use the autohelm if you need to go below: you will probably need to fill in the log every hour, for example. NEVER pee over the side, because of the danger of falling off. Use the heads.

Clipping on

Clip on before you come into the cockpit.

Stay clipped on.

If you need to go forward, clip on to the jackstay.

You must be clipped on when steering too.

A quarter of an hour before the next watch, put on the kettle and make tea. Shake the next person ten minutes before their watch begins.

PART 3: UNDER SAIL

HOW DOES A BOAT SAIL?

Wind is the boat's driving force. The wind flows over the windward side of each sail (causing pressure) and round the leeward side (causing suction).The resulting forces on the sails act in directions A and B, at right angles to the sails.

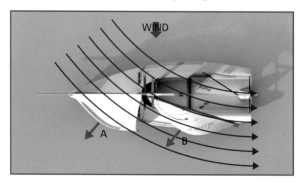

The forces push the boat forwards and sideways. The forward push is welcome! The sideways forces are counteracted by water pressure on the keel, although the boat will always drift sideways a bit.

As the boat heels, the keel begins to exert a righting effect, and the sails' forces decrease. She will automatically heel to exactly the point where the forces are in balance. Note that it is impossible for a yacht to capsize (except in extreme wave conditions) because when she is lying on her side the sails' force is zero and the keel force is maximum. So don't worry about a bit of heeling!

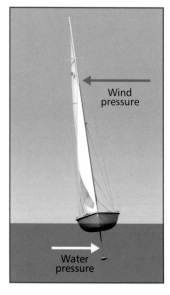

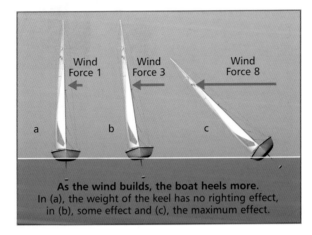

As the wind builds, the boat heels more.
In (a), the weight of the keel has no righting effect,
in (b), some effect and (c), the maximum effect.

Of course, excessive heel is uncomfortable and makes steering difficult so the skipper will show you how to reduce heel, by letting out the sheets or reefing (reducing the sail area).

If the sails are pulled in, forces A and B are almost at right angles to the boat: the sideways force is maximum and the boat will try to heel a lot. When the sails are let out, the forces point forwards so the boat heels less. With the wind behind, there is no heeling effect (but the boat can roll!!!).

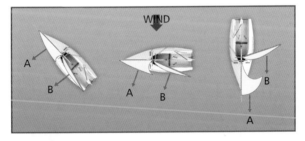

How can I steer?
When the boat is sailing upright, the water flows past the rudder undisturbed. When the rudder is turned, the water is deflected. The water hitting the rudder pushes it, and the back of the boat, in direction C. The bow turns to the left.

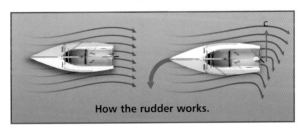

How the rudder works.

How can I stop?

It is the wind in the sails that makes the boat go forward. To stop it or slow down, take the wind out of the sails by either letting out the sheets or by altering course towards the wind, so that the sails flap.

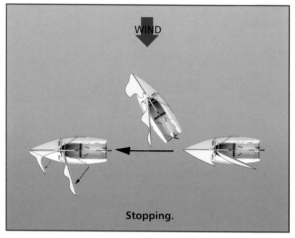

Stopping.

How can I tell which way the wind is blowing?

Everything in sailing is related to wind direction. You can tell which way it's blowing by the feel of it on your cheek, by the wave direction, by the wind indicator at the top of the mast or by the instruments.

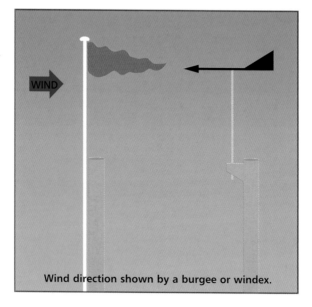

Wind direction shown by a burgee or windex.

Points of sailing

Look at the diagram

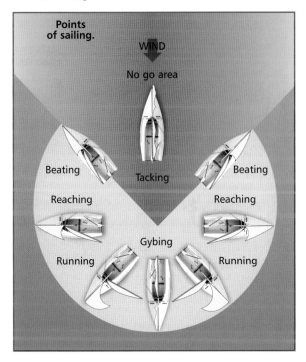

Points of sailing.

WIND

No go area

Beating   Beating

Tacking

Reaching   Reaching

Gybing

Running   Running

There are three points of sailing:

Reaching	– the boat sails across the wind
Beating	– the boat sails towards the wind
Running	– the boat sails away from the wind

Reaching

Here the boat sails at right angles to the wind, which is blowing from the windward side to the leeward side. The sails will be about halfway out.

Beating

If you want to change course towards the wind you must pull in the sails as you turn.

You can go on turning towards the wind until the sails are pulled right in. You are then beating, and in fact are sailing at about 45 degrees to the wind.

If you try to turn further towards the wind, you enter the No Go Area. The sails flap and the boat slows or stops.

If you want to get to a point upwind of your present position, you have to BEAT in a zigzag fashion.

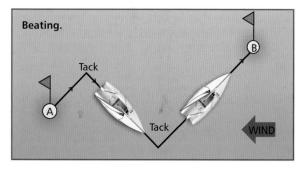

Beating.

At the end of each 'zig' the boat turns through about 90 degrees. This turn is called a TACK. The boat turns 'through' the wind – the sails blow across to the other side. The old genoa sheet is let off and the new one is winched in.

Running

From a reach you may want to change course away from the wind. Let out the sheets as you turn. You can go on turning until the wind is coming from behind the boat. You are RUNNING.

If you turn more, the boat will gybe. The wind gets behind the mainsail and whips it across with a bang, which is potentially dangerous. The best ways to gybe are covered on page 68.

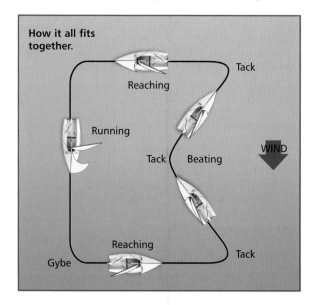

How it all fits together.

RULES OF THE ROAD UNDER SAIL

If you are approaching another sailing boat, the decision about who gives way depends on which tack the boats are on (loosely, which is each boat's windward side).

Starboard tack:	wind coming over starboard side, boom on port side.
Port tack:	wind coming over port side, boom on starboard side.

1. On opposite tacks, port gives way to starboard. Consider easing sheets and passing behind the other boat.

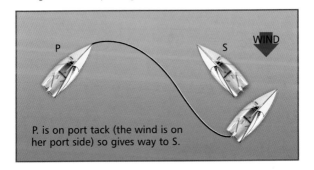

P. is on port tack (the wind is on her port side) so gives way to S.

2. Overlapped, on the same tack, windward gives way to leeward. Turn towards the wind to keep clear.

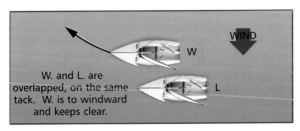

W. and L. are overlapped, on the same tack. W. is to windward and keeps clear.

3. When overtaking, keep clear. You can pass either side, but it is more polite to go to leeward of the other boat.

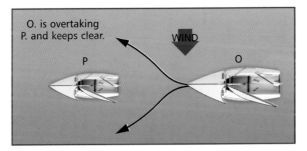

O. is overtaking P. and keeps clear.

If you are approaching a motor vessel

The motor vessel SHOULD give way to you, but you must give way to the following:
A fishing boat
A vessel constrained by its draught, e.g. a vessel that has to stick to the centre of a channel
A vessel restricted in its ability to manoeuvre, e.g. a dredger
A vessel not under command, e.g. with steering breakdown.

Suggested further reading, *Learn the Nautical Rules of the Road.*

WINCHING

On a small boat like a dinghy you are quite safe to hold ropes in your hands. On a yacht you must ALWAYS use a winch to pull in or let out a rope. There could be a force of several tons on the rope and if you simply uncleat it, it will burn through your hands or pull your fingers into the cleat. Always use a winch, even in light winds, to be safe.

Since you will be using the winches all the time, it's worth practising winching even before you set off. Get the skipper to show you how it all works.

Winches are of two types: standard and self-tailing. Nearly all modern yachts are fitted with self-tailing winches. It is possible to use a self-tailing winch as a standard winch.

Ropes must go clockwise round a winch. A quick spin with your hands will remind you which way the rope should be led.

Use a winch handle to wind a winch that is under load. Most winches are geared. Wind clockwise initially and when the handle becomes hard to turn, wind anticlockwise. Winch handles normally lock in place when inserted into a winch. Ask the skipper to show you how to remove the handle as the mechanisms vary.

Self-tailing winches

Self-tailing winches have a gripper arrangement on top. Take three or four clockwise turns of the rope around the winch, starting at the bottom and working upwards with each turn. Put the rope over the metal arm, then pull into the gripper and loop around. You can now let go of the rope and use two hands for winding! If the rope slips, take another turn around the winch. Always watch what is happening at the other end of the rope. A sail may be snagged, and if you keep on winding you could tear it. Always look at what you are pulling in, not at the winch.

1. Put on the turns then lead the rope over the arm and into the jaws.

2. Put in the handle and wind.

Standard Winches

Here we are using a self-tailing winch as a standard winch. Take three or four turns around the winch. There is no gripper to hold the rope, so you must keep tension on yourself. Another crew member can pull the end of the rope for you, this is called 'tailing'. When the sail has been hoisted, sheet pulled in or control line tightened, the rope will need to be secured to a cleat or in a jammer.

1. Take three or four turns clockwise around the drum.

2. Put in the handle and wind.

Letting out a rope

Always use a winch to gradually loosen a rope that is under load. If the rope is secured in a jammer, first wind around the winch three times and secure before lifting the jammer lever. To let a rope off a self-tailer, first free it from the gripper while keeping tension on the rope at all times. Use the palm of your left hand to push the rope anti-clockwise as you gradually ease with your right hand. Keep your fingers clear and do not allow the rope to become slack. Once most of the load has been released, the line can be allowed to run more freely, and eventually the turns can be flicked off entirely.

1. Take out the handle.

2. Take the rope out of the jaws, but keep up the tension with your right hand. Use the palm of your left hand to ease out the rope.

Electric Winches

Electric winches are becoming more common. If you are a beginner, it's best not to use them, because they have no feel and it's easy to wind too far and break something at the other end of the rope. You can always insert a winch handle in an electric winch and wind in the normal way.

If you do use an electric winch, watch carefully what it is doing, i.e. don't look at the button or the winch!

Terminology

If you are lucky, you'll simply be asked to wind in or let out a rope. But people who have done some racing talk about 'on' and 'off', e.g. 'Sheet on!' So be aware this means 'Wind in the sheet, please' (though you'll be lucky to get a please, even when cruising!).

Clearing a riding turn

Sometimes the rope gets jammed.

Tie a second rope to the first with a rolling hitch. Pull on the second rope to take the strain off the jam. Then undo the knitting.

HOISTING SAILS

We will look at how to hoist a mainsail that has been stowed along the boom and unroll a genoa from a roller-reefing furler. Some yachts will have their mainsails furled inside their mast or boom. Racing yachts will often have different headsails that are stowed in bags, then clipped or hanked onto the forestay before hoisting.

Hoisting the mainsail

1. Take off the mainsail cover, fold it up and put it away as directed.
2. Shackle the main halyard to the top of the mainsail. (The halyard is the rope that pulls up the sail)
3. The helmsman will steer the boat into the wind.
4. Make sure the mainsheet is loosened a bit and the kicking strap (vang) is loose. (The kicking strap pulls the boom down.) The topping lift should continue to be tight. (The topping lift pulls the boom up.)
5. Hoist the mainsail. One crew can pull the halyard at the mast while another winches the halyard. This is called sweating the halyard. Alternatively, you can simply winch up the halyard. Watch the sail carefully, rather than looking at the winch. Stop when the halyard reaches its mark, or the luff (front edge) of the sail goes tight.
6. Tighten the kicking strap (vang) and loosen the topping lift slightly.
7. The helmsman can now point the yacht out of the No Go Zone and pull in the mainsheet until the sail stops flapping.

Working as a team to sweat up the mainsail

1. The mast person pulls the halyard sideways.

2. Then the cockpit person pulls in the slack.

3. When the mainsail is up, and the halyard is at its mark, the halyard is secured.

Unwinding the jib or genoa

1. One person keeps some tension on the retrieval line, whilst the other pulls the jibsheet.

2. Then wind in the jibsheet.

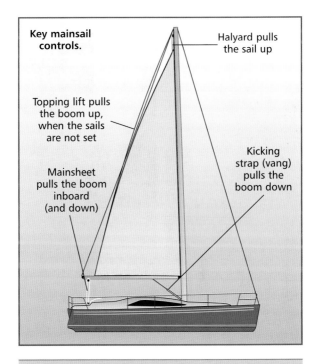

Key mainsail controls.

Halyard pulls the sail up

Topping lift pulls the boom up, when the sails are not set

Kicking strap (vang) pulls the boom down

Mainsheet pulls the boom inboard (and down)

TRIMMING THE SAILS

Let's look at how to trim the sails in moderate winds on a beat, reach and run. Any differences in light and heavy winds are dealt with at the end of each section.

Trimming on a beat

Wind in the leeward genoa sheet using the leeward winch.

To do this take three turns clockwise round the winch. Hold the sheet or, if you are using a self-tailing winch, take the sheet over the metal lead and pull it into the jaws on top of the winch. Then insert the winch handle and wind. As you wind, look up the leech (back edge) of the genoa and continue until the leech is a few inches off the spreader.

Now centralise the mainsheet traveller and pull in the mainsheet. Look at the telltales on the leech of the sail and continue to pull until the top ones stop flying horizontally behind the sail. In light winds you won't need to pull too hard, but in strong winds it may take all your strength.

Now ask the helmsman if the helm is balanced. If he has weather helm (the boat is trying to turn into the wind) drop the traveller to leeward. If he has lee helm, or wants more power, pull the traveller up to windward. The boom should never go to the windward of the boat's centreline.

To trim the mainsheet, watch the mark on the wheel. If the helmsman is having to bear away constantly (turn away from the wind), as here, drop the traveller to leeward until the wheel straightens up.

Trim the genoa by looking at the leech (back edge) while winching. There should be a two inch gap between the leech and the spreader.

TELLTALES

On a beat, the top telltales on the main should stream about half the time. The telltales on the genoa should stream on both sides.

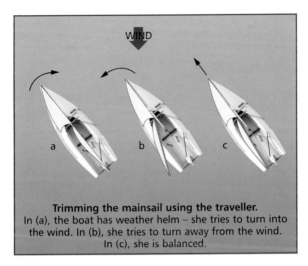

Trimming the mainsail using the traveller.
In (a), the boat has weather helm – she tries to turn into
the wind. In (b), she tries to turn away from the wind.
In (c), she is balanced.

Trimming on a reach

Ease out the genoa sheet until the front of the sail starts to
flap. Alternatively, ease until the windward telltale starts to
misbehave (see diagram). As you ease, look at the sail, not
the winch.

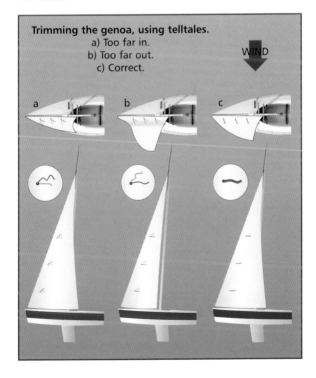

Trimming the genoa, using telltales.
a) Too far in.
b) Too far out.
c) Correct.

To ease the sheet take it out of the cleat or the jaws on top of the winch. Put one hand round the coils, as shown on page 53, and slowly ease out with the other hand. This technique prevents the sheet getting jammed – i.e. prevents a riding turn.

Now put the handle into the winch and wind until the front of the sail just stops flapping. Alternatively, wind until the telltales are streaming on both sides of the genoa. You now have the genoa trimmed nicely, with air flow over both sides of the sail.

Finally, let out the mainsheet until the front of the sail begins to flap, then pull in again until it just stops flapping. The boom will be roughly in line with the Windex.

Trimming on a run

Let out the mainsheet until the boom is against the shroud. (Some skippers like you to pull it a bit further in, to prevent the sail chafing against the shroud and spreaders.) Note that there is no flow around the sail on a run, so the telltales are useless.

In light winds someone can stand with his back to the boom to hold it out, though if the boat is going that slowly the skipper will probably drop the sails and motor.

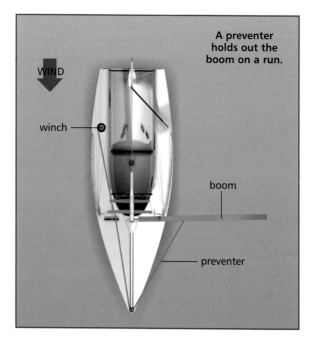

A preventer holds out the boom on a run.

WIND

winch

boom

preventer

In strong winds it's wise to rig a preventer (see diagram).
This holds out the boom as the boat rolls. The preventer
is led aft so it can be released after an accidental gybe.
You must, of course, take it off before a controlled gybe, and
re-rig it on the other side after the gybe.

Setting the genoa is a problem, because it is in the wind
shadow of the mainsail and gets no wind. Often there is
a wind swirl behind the main, and the genoa misbehaves.
You have five options:

1. Try to set the genoa so it is as far out as possible without
   flapping. The more the helmsman steers towards the wind,
   the more the sail will fill.
2. Roll up half the genoa, and then set it as above. At least
   this stops the genoa flapping against the mast fittings.
3. Roll up the genoa completely and sail under
   mainsail alone.
4. Pole out the genoa on the windward side. The easiest way
   to do this is to roll up the genoa. Rig the spinnaker pole as
   shown in the photos, with the windward genoa sheet
   through the jaws on the end of the pole. When all is
   ready, pull the windward sheet to unwind the genoa.
   You are now sailing goosewinged.
5. Set the spinnaker. (See page 72.)

Goosewinging the jib or genoa

1. Roll up the genoa.

2. Put the new sheet through the pole's jaws.

3. Clip the pole to the mast.

4. Hold the pole until the sail is unrolled.

5. The sail now sets nicely on the opposite side to the mainsail.

REEFING

Reefing is making the sails smaller. This makes the boat heel less and balances the helm. You gradually reduce sail as the wind builds.

1. The simplest way to begin is by rolling up a bit of genoa. Let out the genoa sheet just enough so the furling line can be pulled (or winched) in.
2. Then put in the first reef in the mainsail.
   Ask the helmsman to sail on a close reach. Then:
      a. Tighten the topping lift.
      b. Let out the kicking strap (vang).
      c. Slacken the mainsheet slightly.
      d. Let off the main halyard enough for the sail to drop to the first reefing point. The halyard should have been marked to show how far to lower it.
      e. Pull down the first, forward reefing line or go forward and put the cringle (metal eye) onto the reefing hook.
      f. Wind down the first, aft reefing line.
      g. Tighten the halyard, let off the topping lift a little and tighten the kicking strap (vang).
      h. Finally, trim the mainsheet.
3. Put in the second reef.
4. Put in the third reef.

Some boats have in-mast or in-boom reefing for the mainsail. With in-mast reefing you essentially roll the mainsail onto a spindle inside the mast like a giant roller blind. The sail has been specially cut for this, and has vertical battens or no battens at all.

1. The skipper will arrange the topping lift so the boom is at the right angle.
2. Let off the mainsheet a bit.
3. Let off the kicking strap (vang).
4. Pull the furling line. This rolls up some of the mainsail and lets off the outhaul at the same time.

To let out a reef in the genoa, slacken the sheet slightly and at the same time gradually let out the furling line.

To let out a reef in the mainsail first ask the helmsman to sail on a close reach. Then:

1. Let out the mainsheet a little.
2. Take the aft reefing line around a winch and let it out.
3. Let off the kicking strap (vang).
4. Release the halyard a bit.
5. Release the forward reefing line or go forward and take the cringle off the hook.
6. Pull up the halyard, to the mark.
7. Tighten the kicking strap (vang).
8. Trim the mainsheet.

Reefing the mainsail

1. Let off the vang (kicking strap) and the mainsheet a little, and lower halyard to its mark.

2. Winch in the reefing lines.

3. Finally, tighten the halyard and vang, and adjust the mainsheet.

If your boat has a topping lift, tension it before you begin – to prevent the boom from hitting you on the head.

TACKING

During a tack the boat turns slowly 90 degrees 'through' the wind. The mainsail blows across to the new leeward side. The genoa also blows across but you need to release the old genoa sheet and pull in the new one as the boat turns.

The simplest way to handle the mainsail is to leave the sheet cleated throughout. Arrange the traveller lines so the car slides to the correct spot on the new tack, or adjust it after the tack.

WIND

Tacking.

Tacking the genoa with one crew

1. Make sure there is a winch handle handy by the 'new' winch.
2. Make sure the old sheet you will be releasing is not tangled, and the new sheet has a couple of turns on the new winch.
3. Grab the sheet and take a turn off the winch while keeping the tail under tension. Hold this sheet.
4. Reply 'Ready'.
5. The helmsman says 'Lee oh' or 'Lets go' or, if you're unlucky, just turns!
6. Wait until the boat has reached the head-to-wind position.
7. Smartly flick the old sheet off the winch and make sure it has no kinks so it can run out.
8. Pull hard on the new sheet.
9. When you can pull no more, take another turn round the winch. Keep the rope under tension and your fingers clear of the winch.
10. Put in the winch handle and wind.
11. Watch the leech of the genoa. Stop winding when it is a couple of inches off the spreader.
12. Cleat the sheet. Take a bow. You have just made yourself indispensable!

1. Take a sheet in each hand. Let off the old sheet.

2. Pull in the new sheet as the boat turns.

3. Take an extra turn on the winch.

4. Wind the sheet home.

Tacking the genoa with two people

If you are lucky enough to have two people to tack the genoa, one (A) can control the new sheet leaving the other (B) to let off the old sheet, then cross the cockpit and wind the new winch. So have the strongest person on the old sheet to begin with.

The most efficient way to tack is with two people. The person in red pulls in the new sheet, then puts on a further turn, whilst the person in blue lets off the old sheet, brings the handle across the boat and winches in the new sheet.

1. The helmsman warns 'Ready about?'
2. B makes sure there is a winch handle by his side.
3. The crew make sure the old sheet is not tangled, and the new sheet has a couple of turns on the new winch.
4. B takes a turn off the winch and holds this sheet. A holds the new sheet.
5. You both reply 'Ready'.
6. The helmsman says 'Lee oh'.
7. Wait until the boat has reached the head-to-wind position.
8. B smartly flicks the old sheet off the winch and makes sure it has no kinks so it can run out. A pulls hard on the new sheet.
9. When A can pull no more, he takes another turn round the winch and continues pulling.
10. B crosses the boat, puts in the winch handle and winds. With A pulling and B winding the genoa soon comes in.
11. B watches the leech of the genoa and stops winding when it is a couple of inches off the spreader.
12. A can now cleat the sheet.

GYBING

The problem with gybing is that, with the wind behind, the mainsail is constantly powered up and can swing across viciously. The crew's job is to control it. Note that a gybe is quite unlike a tack, where the sails flap harmlessly as the bow turns 'through' the wind.

1. Cleat the traveller.

2. Pull in the mainsheet (on this boat you winch it in).

3. After the gybe, pay out the mainsheet.

4. Let off the old jibsheet and trim the new one.

To make a successful gybe:

1. The helmsman calls 'Ready to gybe?'
2. Take off the boom preventer (if rigged).
3. Pull the mainsheet traveller into the middle of the track, and firmly cleat both control lines. (This is important, or the traveller will shoot across the track in the gybe, catching someone's fingers.)
4. Make sure no-one is near the traveller or the area the mainsheet will traverse.
5. Call 'Ready'.
6. Now pull in all the mainsheet, until the boom is lying down the centreline of the boat, and cleat the mainsheet.
7. The helmsman now calls 'Gybe oh' and bears away until the boom blows across to the new side. Everyone ducks!
8. Meanwhile the new genoa sheet is pulled in, then the old one released.
9. Finally, the mainsheet is slowly paid out so the boom swings out on the new side.
10. Re-rig the boom preventer, if needed.

If it's windy you will need to wear sailing gloves to handle the mainsheet.

The helmsman is an important team member. He needs to steer a steady course just off downwind while the gybe is being set up, then turn slowly and steadily until the wind blows the boom across. Finally, he immediately needs to get back to the proper new course, just off downwind. (The boat may try to skew round onto a reach at this point, which the helmsman must firmly resist.)

Some boats have runners, and this makes things more complicated. Runners are ropes or wires that help support the mast. They have one end attached to the mast near the top of the genoa and the other is secured near the back of the boat. The lower ends have a block and tackle, so each runner can be tightened or loosened.

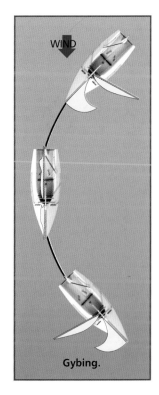

Gybing.

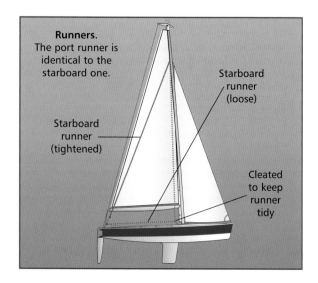

Runners.
The port runner is identical to the starboard one.

Starboard runner (tightened)

Starboard runner (loose)

Cleated to keep runner tidy

When the boat is running with the boom on the port side, the port runner will be slack and the starboard runner tight. As the boom is pulled in to gybe, the port runner is also pulled tight. Before the boom goes across, the starboard runner must be let right off or the boom can't go out on the new side. As a beginner, you may well be given the runners to operate. Talk the procedure through with the skipper before the gybe begins, but the crucial thing is to let off the old runner before the boom comes across!

LOWERING SAILS

At the end of a trip you will normally lower the sails and motor to the marina or anchorage.

1. Firstly, roll up the genoa.
2. Check that there are no ropes over the side, then start the engine and motor slowly ahead.
3. Ease out the kicking strap (vang) and pull up the topping lift a bit. This will prevent the boom dropping when the mainsail comes down.
4. Pull in the mainsheet as the boat turns head-to-wind. Pull it tight and cleat it, or the boom will fly around while you are trying to flake the mainsail along the boom.
5. Check that the main hatch is shut, or you will fall through! Take some sail ties with you onto the coachroof (cabin roof).
6. Go to the mast. Ask for the main halyard to be let off so you can pull down the front edge of the mainsail. (If you're on a big boat, you may need to climb steps on the mast to reach the sail.)
7. Now walk aft along the coachroof and start to concertina the aft end of the mainsail onto the boom.

8. When you have made a few tucks, tie a sail-tie around them and the boom.
9. Repeat, furling the sail and adding sail-ties as you move towards the mast.
10. Finally, take the main halyard off the mainsail and ask where it should be stowed – usually it's shackled to the aft end of the boom. (This stops the halyard flapping against the mast.)

You can usually wait to put on the sail cover(s) until the boat is tied up. Now all you have to do is put out some fenders on each side of the boat, rig the bow and stern lines and enjoy the view as you come into the harbour!

Furling the genoa

1. Uncleat the furling line and genoa sheet.

2. Pull in the furling line, making sure the sheet runs out freely. Finally coil up the furling line.

Dropping the main

1. Let off the halyard.

2. Pull down the sail.

3. Shut the hatch.

4. Take the sail ties with you.

5. Concertina the sail
and hold it in place with
the sail ties.

6. Work forward from
the end of the boom
to the mast.

SPINNAKERS

Although a spinnaker is trouble waiting to happen, once it's
up and pulling you will have a memorable ride. One way to
avoid problems is to pack the spinnaker properly in its bag,
or it will come out twisted.

Packing the spinnaker

Take the spinnaker below and make sure you have the bag
to hand. You will also need three short lengths of rope.

1. Tie the head of the spinnaker to a grabrail.
   (The head must say HEAD – otherwise it's easy to get
   the wrong corner.)
2. Run your hand down one edge of the sail to make sure
   there are no twists.
3. Tie this corner of the spinnaker to another grabrail.
4. Run your hand along the next edge of the sail.
5. Tie the third corner of the sail to a grabrail. The corners
   are now well separated with the bulk of the sail hanging
   between.
6. Put the bag under the sail and bundle the spinnaker into it.
7. Untie the three corners and tie them so they are poking
   out of the bag radially, and can't get twisted.
8. Finally, close the lid of the bag.

If you pack the sail correctly, when you come to hoist the
spinnaker you can shackle on the sheets and halyard to the
correct corners and know the sail will go up without a twist!

Definitions

Look at the diagram:

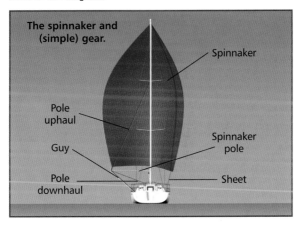

The spinnaker and (simple) gear.

Spinnaker

Pole uphaul

Guy

Pole downhaul

Spinnaker pole

Sheet

You will see that the pole is on the opposite side to the boom.

The pole is held up by an uphaul, and down by a downhaul.
Both need to be tight, to stop the pole bouncing up and
down.

The guy goes from a winch in the cockpit, through the end of
the pole and to the windward corner of the spinnaker. The
pole spreads out the spinnaker. When you winch the guy aft it
pulls the spinnaker and the pole around to the windward side.

The sheet goes from the cockpit to the leeward corner of
the spinnaker. It works like the sheet on any sail – you let it
out until the sail curls, then pull it in until the sail just fills.

The halyard goes from the top corner of the spinnaker to a pulley up the mast, then down and back to a winch. The halyard pulls up the spinnaker.

Lazy sheets and guys

On a large yacht you will have a sheet and a guy on each side - i.e. four ropes in all - (see diagram below). Only one rope on each side of the boat is used at a time.

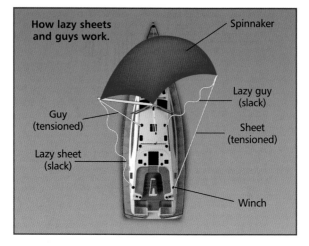

How lazy sheets and guys work.

Spinnaker

Lazy guy (slack)

Guy (tensioned)

Sheet (tensioned)

Lazy sheet (slack)

Winch

In the diagram the guy is tight on the port side, and the port sheet is loose. This is called the lazy sheet.

On the starboard side the sheet is tensioned and the lazy guy is loose.

The two guys and two sheets mean:

A. The lead for each guy is forward, which helps pull down on the windward corner of the spinnaker.

B. The lead for each sheet is aft which allows the leeward side of the spinnaker to fly.

C. When gybing the spinnaker, you take the tension on both sheets. This gives slack guys, which is very useful when trying to get the pole end off one and onto the other.

If it all goes wrong

What would you do if someone fell overboard when the spinnaker was up and drawing? It would take ages to get the thing down and get back to the victim.

On my boat we have a rule that there are no stopper knots in the ends of the sheets and guys or the halyard. If we get in a real mess we can let all these ropes go and the spinnaker (trailing the ropes) will just blow away. Then we can go back for our friend.

Hoisting the spinnaker

The spinnaker is hoisted behind the genoa and in the lee of the mainsail. These two sails shield it from the wind on its way aloft.

1. Decide which side the pole will be set. This is usually the windward side, or on a run the opposite side to the mainsail.
2. Take the spinnaker bag forward and clip it to the leeward guardrail. (Otherwise it will fall over the side after the hoist.)
3. Clip the sheet to its corner of the sail.
4. Take the guy outside the windward shroud, round the forestay and back to the bag. Clip the guy onto its corner of the spinnaker.
5. Make sure the halyard runs outside everything and clip it onto the head of the spinnaker.

Now set up the pole

A. Attach the uphaul and downhaul to the pole before you move it from its mountings. The ropes will prevent the pole falling overboard if you drop it.
B. Clip the pole to the mast.
C. Clip the guy through the jaws at the outer end of the pole.
D. Call back to the cockpit for them to raise the pole until it's horizontal.

Now for the hoist.

1. The helmsman will bear away onto a broad reach/run.
   This enables the main and genoa to blanket the
   spinnaker on its way up.
2. Pull back on the guy so one corner of the sail is pulled
   out of the bag and up to the forestay.
3. Wind the guy back a little more so the pole is off
   the forestay.
4. On the command 'Hoist' pull up the spinnaker. Do not
   pull in the sheet yet – you don't want the sail to fill on
   its way up.
5. If the spinnaker starts to wrap round the forestay, the
   helmsman luffs a little to get a bit of air into it.
6. Finally, when the sail is fully up, pull in the sheet until
   the sail fills. Then roll up the genoa.

Trimming the spinnaker

Start with the pole.

- Set the height of the pole so the two lower corners
  of the spinnaker are the same height above the deck.
  Raise the outboard end of the pole by letting off the
  downhaul and winching up the uphaul, and vice-versa
  to lower the pole.

- Set the angle of the pole fore and aft by letting off
  the sheet and winding in the guy to swing the pole
  aft. The pole should be at right angles to the wind
  i.e. at right angles to the Windex. This spreads the
  sail so it can catch the most wind.

Then trim the sail in the normal way using the sheet.

- Let out the sheet until the windward edge of the
  spinnaker begins to curl.

- Wind in the sheet until the curl settles down
  i.e. the sail just fills.

- Keep letting out a bit of sheet and winding it back
  in to keep the sail as far out as you can without it
  flapping.

- If the wind shifts and you can't wind in the sheet
  fast enough to keep the sail full, ask the helmsman
  to bear away to help you.

Gybing the spinnaker

Ask if you are doing an end-for-end gybe or
a dip-pole gybe.

End-for-end gybe with one sheet and one guy

1. The helmsman bears away onto a run.
2. Wind in the mainsheet so the boom lies along the centreline of the boat.
3. Clip yourself on to the jackstay and move to the mast.
4. Unclip the pole from the mast and clip it to the new guy. The pole is now across the boat, suspended from the two guys.
5. Unclip the other end of the pole from the guy and clip the pole onto the mast. If there is too much pressure ask someone in the cockpit to ease out a little on the pole uphaul.
6. Trim the spinnaker and let out the mainsheet so the boom goes out on the new side.

End-for-end gybe with two sheets and two guys

First, take the pressure on the two sheets. Ease out the two guys. Then gybe as above.

Dip-pole gybe with two sheets and two guys

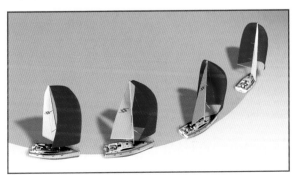

The idea is that the outer end of the pole is lowered, the guy is released from the jaws of the pole, the pole swings across the foredeck, is clipped to the new guy and raised to the horizontal again.

The only problem is that the pole is too long to swing across so it is first slid up the mast to improve the geometry.

1. The helmsman bears away onto a run.
2. Wind in the mainsheet until the boom is central.
3. Take the pressure on the two sheets and slacken the two guys.
4. Push the spinnaker pole up the mast track.
5. Ask for the pole uphaul to be slackened slowly.
6. Unclip the guy from the jaws of the pole.
7. Swing the pole across to the new side.
8. Put the new guy into the pole's jaws.
9. Slide the pole down the mast.
10. Ask for the pole to be raised using the uphaul.
11. Trim the spinnaker and let out the mainsheet so the boom goes out on the new side.

Lowering the spinnaker

Before you begin make sure all the spinnaker sheets and guys and the halyard are free of tangles and ready to run.

Position someone on the spinnaker halyard, someone on the guy and someone on the leeward deck ready to pull in on the sheet and bring the spinnaker down into the cockpit or down the hatch.

If you are very shorthanded you may need to put the boat on autohelm so the helmsman can come forward and handle the guy and the halyard.

1. Unfurl the genoa.
2. When everyone is ready, the helmsman bears away onto a run.
3. Pull in the sheet and grab it between the sail and the deck, getting ready to pull like crazy as the sail comes down.
4. Release the guy and then the halyard. The spinnaker will swing behind the mainsail and start to drop.
5. Pull the sail inboard and stuff it down the hatch.
6. When it's all below unclip the sheets and guys and halyard and tidy them up. Then clip on and go forward and put the pole away. On your way aft bring back the spinnaker bag.
7. Finally, go below and pack the spinnaker into the bag.

GENNAKERS

A gennaker is a downwind sail that is, indeed, a cross between a spinnaker and a genoa (see diagram).

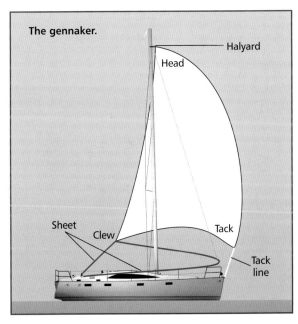

The gennaker.

The tack of the gennaker is attached right at the front of the boat.

The two sheets are rigged like the sheets of a genoa, but led so the sail can be gybed across in front of the forestay.

Often, a gennaker is hoisted from a sock. The diagram shows how this works.

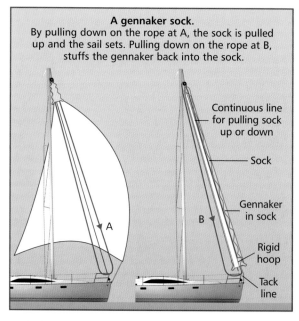

A gennaker sock.
By pulling down on the rope at A, the sock is pulled up and the sail sets. Pulling down on the rope at B, stuffs the gennaker back into the sock.

Continuous line for pulling sock up or down

Sock

Gennaker in sock

Rigid hoop

Tack line

Hoisting

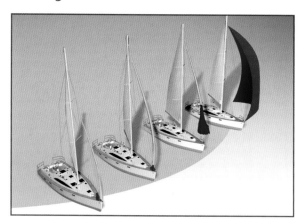

1. Get the sail on deck in its sock.
2. Attach the tack line.
3. Attach the sheets.
4. Attach the top of the sock to the halyard and pull up the sail in its sock.
5. The helmsman bears away onto a run.
6. Pull the sock line so the sock rises and the gennaker is exposed.
7. Trim the sheet to set the gennaker.

Gybing

As the mainsail is gybed, let off the old gennaker sheet and pull in the new one.

Dropping the gennaker

1. Turn onto a run.
2. Ease out the gennaker sheet a bit.
3. Pull down on the sock line so the gennaker is stuffed into the sock.
4. When it's doused, lower the whole thing onto the deck, unclip it and take it below.

PART 4: MAYDAY AND MAN OVERBOARD (MOB)

MAYDAY

Sending a Mayday call

If your situation is such that life may be lost, send a Mayday call on channel 16.

1. You will need to know where you are. Use one of the following:
   a. Look at the chart and see roughly where the boat is e.g. '170 degrees true FROM Beachy Head, 7 miles'.
   b. Look at the GPS or chart plotter and read the latitude and longitude e.g. '50 degrees 22 decimal 47 minutes north, 001 degrees 26 decimal 80 east'.
2. Switch on the radio at the control panel and at the set.
3. Select channel 16.
4. Press the 1w/25w button until 25w is displayed.
5. Turn the squelch until a hiss is heard, then turn it back until the hiss just disappears.
6. Pick up the handset.
7. Press and hold down the Press To Talk button and say

'Mayday Mayday Mayday
This is yacht...............yacht..............yacht................
Mayday yacht ....
Our position is ....
We are sinking/ have a man overboard/ are on fire/ etc.
Immediate assistance required e.g. tow/ search and rescue/ etc
Four people on board
Other useful information: e.g. we have a liferaft and are abandoning ship into it
Over'

8. Release the PTT switch and wait for the reply.
9. If none comes, repeat the Mayday call.

1. Switch on the VHF at the control panel.

2. Switch on the set.

3. Set the squelch.

4. Press channel 16.

5. Pick up the mike. Press to talk.

6. Release the switch to listen.

Sending a Mayday on a DSC set

A set with Digital Selective Calling (DSC) has a red button under a red cover. Using this facility before sending a voice Mayday doubles your chances of being located, because the set first sends a short burst of information containing your boat's details and your position.

1. Switch on the set at the control panel and at the set itself.
2. Slide and hold back the red cover.
3. Press the red button once.
4. Then press and hold down the red button.
5. The set will count down and tell you the alert has been sent.
6. Wait 15 seconds, and the screen should show an acknowledgement.
7. In any case, after 15 seconds pick up the microphone and send a voice Mayday call i.e.
   Mayday, Mayday, Mayday
   This is .... etc etc, see above.

If you need your call sign, it is often on a label by the radio. Or you can write it here:

Remember, the coastguard would rather hear about problems early than deal with emergencies later.

Mayday relay

If your radio has a greater range than the vessel in distress, you may need to rebroadcast a Mayday you have received.

Re-broadcast the mayday message without any changes

16

"Mayday relay, Mayday relay, Mayday relay. This is Yacht Sierra, Sierra, Sierra. MMSI 234780510. Mayday received from motor cruiser Swift. Mayday Swift MMSI 233077310. Position Black Rocks, Deadly Point. Aground and breaking up. Require immediate assistance. Two persons on board."

DSC distress alert

1. Open the red cover.

2. Press red button.

3. Select cause of distress, if time.

4. Press and hold the red button through the countdown.

5. Wait no more than 15 seconds for the acknowledgement.
Send voice Mayday on channel 16 using high power.

For speed
1. Open cover.
2. Press red button. Release.
3. Press and hold red button for 5 seconds.

MAN OVERBOARD (MOB)

Soon after you set off the skipper may give a demonstration of the MOB procedure. This varies from boat to boat and of course depends whether you are sailing or motoring (which gives an easier recovery). Here is a rough plan for a fully-crewed yacht which is sailing. I've followed it with suggestions for the toughest scenario – when there are just the two of you and the skipper goes over the side.

The first point to make about falling off is – DON'T. If there is any possibility of this disaster, everyone should be in lifejackets and harnesses and clipped on. The RNLI advice is to wear lifejackets at all times. They also caution that this is a Mayday scenario. Send a Mayday immediately; don't wait while you spend half an hour trying to recover the casualty. If you do recover him, you can always cancel the Mayday.

MOB procedure for a fully crewed yacht

Five things should happen simultaneously:
1. Shout 'Man Overboard'.
2. Tack, without touching the genoa sheet. This stops the boat dead, in the hove-to position.
3. One person is delegated to point at the MOB throughout the rescue, so you don't lose him.
4. Send a Mayday.
5. Press the MOB Button on the GPS. The machine will give a bearing and distance back to this position (but be aware that the MOB may drift down tide, away from the designated spot).
6. Throw the MOB a lifebuoy or use the throwing line or, in extremis, chuck anything that will help him float.

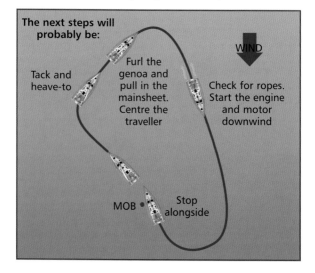

The next steps will probably be:

WIND

Tack and heave-to

Furl the genoa and pull in the mainsheet. Centre the traveller

Check for ropes. Start the engine and motor downwind

MOB • Stop alongside

7. Furl the genoa.
8. Check that there are no ropes overboard.
9. Start the engine.
10. Consider lowering the mainsail.
11. Motor back to the MOB.
12. If you have a lifesling, launch it and circle the victim.

Finally, you will have to retrieve the MOB.
There are several methods:

A. Rig a recovery line from a forward cleat to a sheet winch. The casualty steps on it, then is raised slowly as you winch. Don't trap their fingers or toes!
B. With the boat alongside the MOB, cut the lines tensioning the guardrail and try to drag him aboard.
C. Give him a line and gently pull him to the stern, where he may be able to climb aboard using the bathing ladder. Make sure the propeller is stationary.
D. Launch the dinghy and pull him aboard that. The liferaft can be used in an emergency.
E. Rig up a block and tackle and winch him up, or lead a halyard to the windlass.

Whichever is the preferred method on your boat, the key thing is to have practised it.

Shorthanded procedure

If the skipper has gone over the side and you are left on your own, you will be too busy to carry out all the steps above.

1. Stop the boat by tacking.
2. Keep an eye on the MOB.
3. Send a Mayday.
4. If there is not too much wind and you have a lifesling, consider deploying it and sailing round the MOB until he catches the sling. Then stop and draw him slowly alongside.
5. If it's windy, throw the danbuoy and lifebuoy, furl the genoa, check for ropes and start the engine. Consider dropping the mainsail. Manoeuvre alongside and retrieve the MOB.
6. The Mayday can be cancelled when he is safely on board.

If the skipper has fallen off while you were asleep, send a Mayday immediately. Turn the boat through 180 degrees and retrace your steps on a reciprocal course.

If the skipper is unconscious, don't get into the water yourself. Do what you can from the yacht, and wait for help.

PART 5: NAVIGATION

You may feel that navigation is someone else's job. After all, the skipper will usually brief you on where you're going, plan the legs, draw the course on the chart, set up the waypoints on the chartplotter, and give you a Course To Steer. All you have to do is follow it, right?

Well, you could do that. But wouldn't it be better to have an understanding of how a chart works, what latitude and longitude are, how the tide behaves and what depth of water you can expect along your route? Plus it would be helpful to know about the compass and how buoys are used to keep the boat safe.

With a bit of basic navigational knowledge you will enjoy the trip more and be able to contribute. Plus the skipper will sleep more soundly when you are on watch!

HOW A CHART WORKS

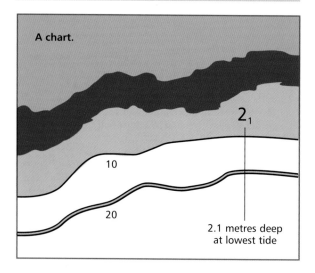

A chart.

2_1

10

20

2.1 metres deep
at lowest tide

A chart is like a map. The land is shown in yellow and the sea in blue, with different colours for increasing depth. Areas that are covered with water at high tide but are land at low tide are coloured green.

The contours show the depth of water at the lowest tide you are likely to experience. So if it says 2.1, for example, it means the depth should be at least 2.1 metres.

Tide tables give the 'extra' depth of water on top of the charted depth. So if, for example, the tide table says that today the height of tide is 4.3 metres at noon, then at our previous spot at noon the depth of water should be 2.1 + 4.3 = 6.4 metres. If our boat draws 2.1 metres there will be 4.3 metres of water under the keel.

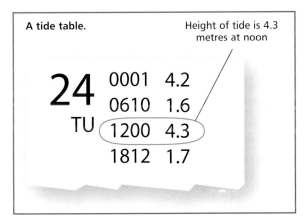

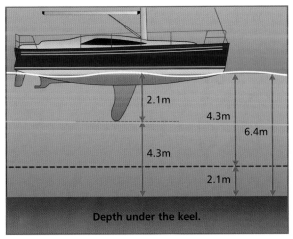

The chart is aligned with true north at the top. (We will see in a minute that the compass in front of the helmsman does not, sadly, point towards true north, but it's usually not too far off.) For the moment, just find the compass rose which will be on some uncrowded part of the chart.

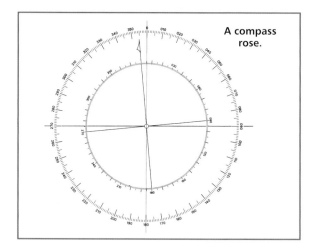

A compass rose.

Along the vertical sides of the chart is the latitude scale. A position on the chart represents a position on the earth's surface and the measurement is in degrees from the equator. For example, a latitude of 50°N is somewhere on the circle shown in the diagram. Each degree is split into 60 minutes, and each minute represents a nautical mile. So you can use the latitude scale to help you measure distance on the chart.

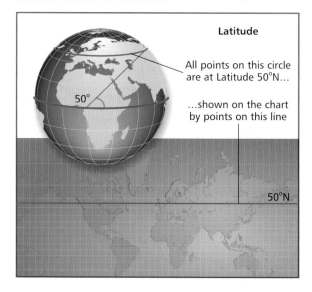

Latitude

All points on this circle are at Latitude 50°N…

50°

…shown on the chart by points on this line

50°N

Along the top of the chart is the longitude scale. This is a measure of your distance east or west of the meridian (line) through Greenwich. For example: 10°E means that you are somewhere on the line shown on the diagram.

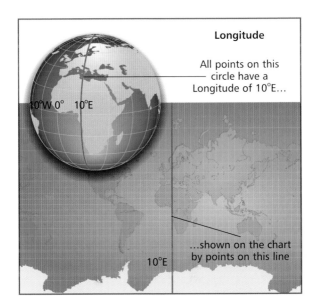

Combining latitude and longitude gives your position.
For example 50°N 10°E is as shown on the diagram.

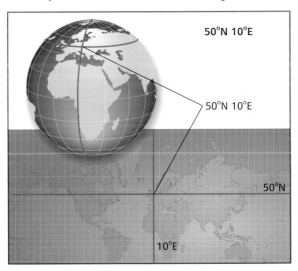

You will want to give your position more precisely than this
e.g. 50° 22' .47N 10° 26' .80E means 50° and 22.47 minutes N,
10° and 26.8 minutes east.

Knowing this is useful because the GPS set on the boat gives
your position in just this way i.e. in lat and long.

CHART SYMBOLS

Admiralty Chart 5011 is actually a book showing all the chart symbols. Here, we will just concentrate on some common dangers, such as rocks and shallows. You must know these.

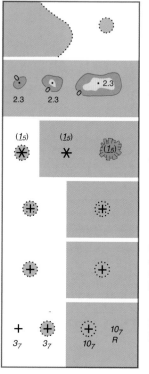

Danger line: draws attention to symbol

Rocks which do not cover, with height above high water (usually MHWS)

Rocks which cover and uncover with height above Chart Datum

Rocks awash at Chart Datum

Underwater rocks, dangerous to surface navigation.
Depth unspecified.

Underwater rock.
Depth below Chart Datum.

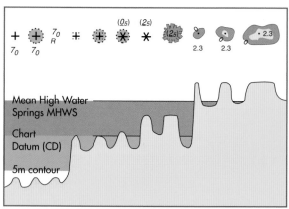

Mean High Water Springs MHWS

Chart Datum (CD)

5m contour

Some other chart symbols denoting danger

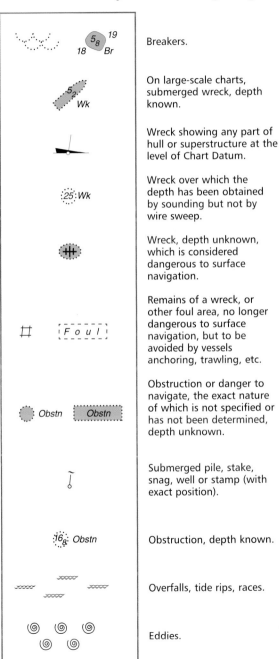

Breakers.

On large-scale charts, submerged wreck, depth known.

Wreck showing any part of hull or superstructure at the level of Chart Datum.

Wreck over which the depth has been obtained by sounding but not by wire sweep.

Wreck, depth unknown, which is considered dangerous to surface navigation.

Remains of a wreck, or other foul area, no longer dangerous to surface navigation, but to be avoided by vessels anchoring, trawling, etc.

Obstruction or danger to navigate, the exact nature of which is not specified or has not been determined, depth unknown.

Submerged pile, stake, snag, well or stamp (with exact position).

Obstruction, depth known.

Overfalls, tide rips, races.

Eddies.

THE COMPASS

Variation

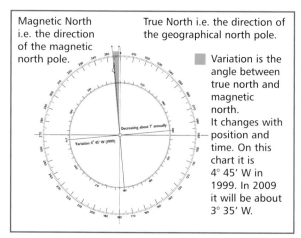

Magnetic North i.e. the direction of the magnetic north pole.

True North i.e. the direction of the geographical north pole.

Variation is the angle between true north and magnetic north.
It changes with position and time. On this chart it is 4° 45' W in 1999. In 2009 it will be about 3° 35' W.

Decreasing about 7' annually

Variation 4° 45' W (1999)

Deviation

Theoretically the needle in a magnetic compass points to magnetic north, but the compass in most boats is subject to magnetic interference from the engine, the electrics and electronics. Any error caused is known as deviation.

- Deviation is the angle between a magnetic bearing and the same bearing taken by a particular compass in a particular boat.
- Unlike variation, deviation varies according to the boat's heading. To see why this is, imagine that all the 'interference' in a boat behaves as though it is concentrated into a fixed iron block.

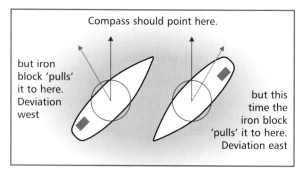

Compass should point here.

but iron block 'pulls' it to here. Deviation west

but this time the iron block 'pulls' it to here. Deviation east

In practice deviation is often reduced to a minimum or removed altogether by a compass adjuster. He will swing the compass to find out the deviation on various headings, then place magnets to remove or reduce it. He will then produce a Deviation Table for you.

Converting bearings

1. For the order of converting types of bearing simply remember the mnemonic: <u>T</u>rue <u>V</u>irgins <u>M</u>ake <u>D</u>ull <u>C</u>ompanions.

	Variation		Deviation	
True	◄——►	**Magnetic**	◄—►	**Compass**

2. Error West, Compass Best, i.e. compass reads bigger.

T	**v**	**M**	**d**	**C**
	◄— W = –			

If going to the left along the row, subtract westerly deviation or variation. Add easterly deviation or variation. If going to the right, add westerly error. Subtract easterly error.

Example: Compass gives bearing 090°. Deviation 4° W. Variation 3° W. What is True bearing?

T	**v**	**M**	**d**	**C**
083	-3	086	-4	090

Answer 083° T

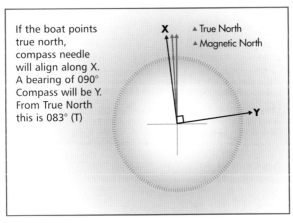

If the boat points true north, compass needle will align along X. A bearing of 090° Compass will be Y. From True North this is 083° (T)

X　▲ True North
　　▲ Magnetic North
————————►Y

Example: True bearing 130°. Variation 5° W. Deviation 3° E. What is Compass bearing?

T	**v**	**M**	**d**	**C**
W – ◄——		——► W +		
130(T)	+5	=135(M)	-3 =	132(C)

Error is the sum of Variation and Deviation.

With a handbearing compass, cautiously assume deviation is zero. Check by continuously taking a bearing with the handbearing compass on a distant object, while turning the boat through 360°.

BUOYAGE

IALA buoyage

The system of bouyage, including standard shapes, colours etc and used throughout Europe is known as the IALA system, (International Association of Lighthouse Authorities).

DIRECTION OF BUOYAGE - a starboard hand buoy marks the starboard side of the channel when entering harbour. This direction is usually obvious, but where any doubt may exist, this symbol shows the direction of buoyage.

IALA System A

Lateral marks
Port hand
Light: red,
any rhythm.

Starboard hand.
Light: green,
any rhythm.

Modified Lateral Mark
You **could** go either side, but one is preferred.
  Preferred channel to starboard   Preferred channel to port

Isolated Danger Mark
Light: White Fl(2)
Isolated danger with
clear water all round.

Safe Water Mark
Light: Isophase or occulting or 1
long flash every 10 seconds or
Morse 'A'(- —). Usually placed
at the approach to a channel -
shows safe water all round.

Special Mark
Not a navigational mark but indicating a special feature.
Light (when fitted): Yellow. Any characteristic that does
not conflict with nav. marks. May be any shape, topmark
(if any): Yellow X.

IALA System B

Lateral buoys in the USA

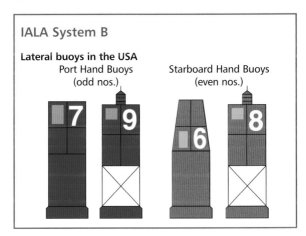

Port Hand Buoys (odd nos.)   Starboard Hand Buoys (even nos.)

In the USA the buoyage system for entering harbour is different from most other places.

Cardinal marks

Cardinal buoys indicate the direction in which a particular danger lies, and the side on which it is safe to pass.

- A north cardinal lies to the north of the danger, and the clear water is to the north of the buoy.
- The characteristics of the light refer to the figures on a clock face. (LFl = long flash.)

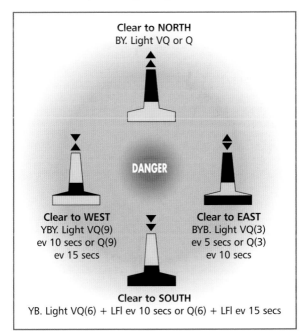

Clear to NORTH
BY. Light VQ or Q

DANGER

Clear to WEST
YBY. Light VQ(9)
ev 10 secs or Q(9)
ev 15 secs

Clear to EAST
BYB. Light VQ(3)
ev 5 secs or Q(3)
ev 10 secs

Clear to SOUTH
YB. Light VQ(6) + LFl ev 10 secs or Q(6) + LFl ev 15 secs

KEEPING A LOG

DATE FRIDAY 27 July   **FROM** _____ Denhaven to L'Aberpêche

1 **2** **3** **4** ... **9**

| TIME BST | COURSE ORDERED (°C) | LOG READING | ESTIMATED | | | WIND | SEA | WEATHER | Vis | Bar | POSITION | SOURCE OF FIX | NEXT WP |
			COURSE STEERED	DIST RUN	LEEWAY								
0700	⚓	–	–	–	–	NW3	Calm	0/8	G	15	Denhaven Hr	Vis	–
0800	Var	–	Var	–	–	„	„	„	„	„	„ entrance	Vis	1
0900	250	2·7	250	2·7	3°	„	slight	„	„	15½	Griddle Pier	Vis	4
1000	„	6·5	„	3·8	„	NW4	mod	„	„	„	54°11'·2 N : 01°13'·4 E	RN	„
1100	„	10·9	„	4·3	4°	„	„	„	„	„	54°10'·1 N : 01°10'·5 E	„	„
1200	185	15·8	190	4·7	NIL	„	„	„	„	16	54°06'·2 N : 01°09'·4 E	„	29
1300	„	20·6	„	4·7	„	„	„	„	„	„	54°01'·1 N : 01°08'·7 E	„	„
1400	„	25·6	„	4·9	„	„	„	„	3/8 H	„	53°55'·0 N : 01°07'·3 E	„	„
1500	„	29·7	185	4·1	5°	WS	„	„	„	17	53°52'·2 N : 01°05'·2 E	„	„

REMARKS **5**

HW Dover 0856   LW 1603

0740 start engine
0750 Slip under power. Co + Sp to clear Hr – WP1 Dep Fix
0805 WP1 a/c 240. set full main + Gen. Sp 3kts. Set Log 0 Stop engine **6**
0830 Bench Bn → 1'. L1·2. 0855 Griddle Pier ↦ ½' L 2·5 a/c 250
0915 Wind inc. furl gen
0925 TS now fair

1115 WP4 a/c 185   L 12·0. unfurl gen **7**

1230   Fix NN

1520 WP 29 a/c 160   L 34·8 **8**

It should be possible to plot a vessel's position at any time
from the information in the log. Use a new page for each day.

1. Work in BST.
2. Work in degrees Compass and convert for chartwork.
3. Log gives distance run.
4. Estimate course steered.
5. HW and LW at relevant port.
6. Note landmarks and record them.
7. Record sail changes (affect leeway).
8. Record changes of course: especially when tacking.
9. Watch for changes in barometric pressure - reassess
   plan if more than 3.5 mb change in 3 hours
   (rising/falling quickly).

From _Logbook for
Cruising Under Sail_ by
John Mellor/Wiley Nautical.

RECOGNISING LIGHTS, SHAPES AND SOUND SIGNALS

A vessel must give way to any vessel above it in the list, except in narrow channels, traffic separation schemes and when overtaking. In other words:

A vessel under power gives way to:
- a vessel not under command (NUC).
- a vessel restricted in ability to manoeuvre (RAM).
- a vessel engaged in fishing.
- a sailing vessel (but see below).

A sailing vessel must keep clear of:
- a vessel not under command (NUC).
- a vessel restricted in ability to manoeuvre (RAM).
- a vessel constrained by draft (CBD).
- a vessel engaged in fishing.

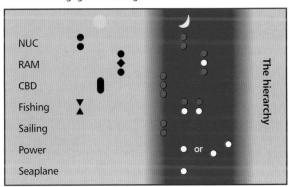

The hierarchy

NUC
RAM
CBD
Fishing
Sailing
Power
Seaplane

Small craft - large ships

The Rules may say that, with the exceptions shown above, power gives way to sail. But in practice this increasingly applies only to power boats and small commercial vessels.
- Large commercial vessels cannot stop or alter course quickly. A laden tanker may travel several miles after she has stopped her engines.
- Commercial vessels are now often travelling fast. The time between another ship being a comfortable distance away, and being dangerously close, can be unexpectedly short.
- Small craft can be hard to see from the bridge of a large vessel, especially when the bridge is aft.

Generally small craft should keep clear of large commercial vessels both in confined water and in the open sea - but always making it clear beyond doubt that they are getting out of the way.

Restricted visibility (Rule 19)
a) Proceed at safe speed adapted to visibility.
b) When using radar, also maintain listening watch.
c) Keep clear of shipping lanes and channels.

Lights and shapes

The lights shown by various vessels fit into two categories:

a) Navigation lights. These are the lights that any vessel must show from sunset to sunrise and also in restricted visibility. They vary according to a vessel's size and there are different lights for vessels under power and under sail.

b) Distinguishing lights (and shapes). In addition to showing navigation lights, vessels employed in certain activities (eg towing or fishing) or in certain situations (eg not under command) also show distinguishing lights by night and shapes by day. For this reason it is logical to list shapes and distinguishing lights together.

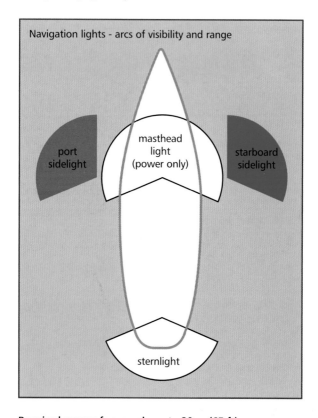

Navigation lights - arcs of visibility and range

port sidelight

masthead light (power only)

starboard sidelight

sternlight

Required ranges for vessels up to 20 m (65 ft)

YACHT SIZE	7m - 12m	12m - 20m
Tricolour lantern	2 miles	2 miles
Masthead light	2 miles	3 miles
Side lights	1 mile	2 miles
Stern light	2 miles	2 miles

Power-driven vessels underway (Rule 23)

Stern   Side   Bow

Over 50 m

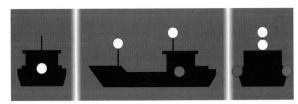

Masthead light – second masthead light aft and higher – sidelights – sternlight.

Under 50 m

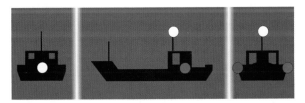

Masthead light – sidelights and sternlight.

Under 12 m

May show all-round white light (instead of masthead light and sternlight) + sidelights.

Under 7 m & speed under 7 knots

May show all-round white light only.

Vessels under sail (Rule 25)

Stern   Side   Bow

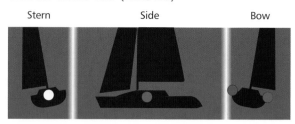

Sidelights & sternlight only – no masthead light.

Under 20m may have combined masthead lantern
(red/green/white) with no other lights.

(Rare) A yacht may carry an all-round red over green, plus side
and stern lights.

A sailing yacht when motor sailing shows the same lights
as a power vessel. So engine on, masthead lights on.

By day: Sailing vessels
using their engines for
propulsion but with sails
hoisted should show forward
a cone, point down.

Vessels at anchor (Rule 30)

Under 50 m   **Over 50 m**

All round white light forward.

A second white light aft (lower than for'd light).

By day: one ball.

Note: Yachts over 7 m must display an anchor light.
Under 7 m need not, unless near a fairway or anchorage.

Vessels aground

Stern   Side   Bow

 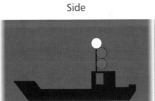 

Under 50 m: two all round red lights plus anchor light.

 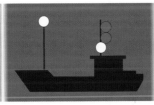 

Over 50 m: two all round red lights, plus anchor lights.

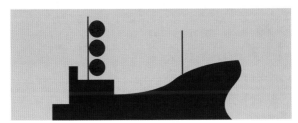

Three vertical balls.

Note: vessels under 12 m need not exhibit lights or shapes when aground.

Towing (Rule 24)

The tow is measured from the stern of the tug to the stern of the tow.

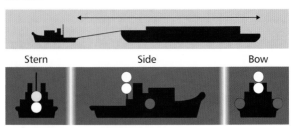

Stern   Side   Bow

Tug's lights when tow is less than 200 m.

Tug's lights when tow is more than 200 m.

If the tug is more than 50 m it will also carry a second (white) masthead light aft of, and higher than, the forward one.

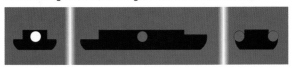

Vessel being towed.

By day: Diamonds only needed if tow exceeds 200 m.

Vessels not under command (Rule 27)
(eg with mechanical or steering breakdown).

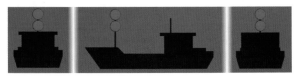

Two clearly visible all round red lights.
Note: although it is unlikely that a vessel not under command would be using her engines, she would, if making way, show navigation lights as well as NUC lights.

By day:
two balls.

Vessels restricted in their ability to manoeuvre (Rule 27) (eg dredgers, tugs)

Stern   Side   Bow

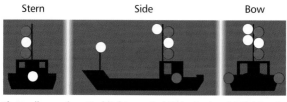

Three all-round vertical lights: red/white/red, plus sidelights etc. if making way).

By day, three vertical shapes: ball/diamond/ball.

A working **dredger** shows two vertical red lights on obstructed side and two vertical green lights on clear side - as well as Restricted in Ability to Manoeuvre lights (and navigation lights if making way).

By day: two vertical balls on obstructed (working) side, and two diamonds on side where it is clear to pass, in addition to restricted in ability to manoeuvre shapes.

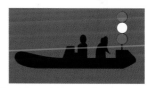

Diving tender. Flag 'A' or rigid replica. Although diving tenders rarely operate at night, when doing so they must show the vertical red/white/red lights indicating restricted in ability to manoeuvre.

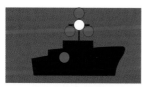

Mine clearance vessels exhibit three all round green lights or balls, plus lights for power vessel or lights/shapes for anchored vessel. Do not approach this vessel within 1000 m.

Vessel constrained by draught (Rule 28)

Stern   Side   Bow

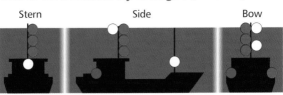

Vessel constrained by draught (eg a vessel confined to the centre of a channel) shows three vertical all-round red lights as well as normal navigation lights. By day a vertical cylinder.

Fishing vessels (Rule 26)

Vessel trawling (ie towing some kind of net):
All-round green over white lights. Show regular navigation lights when making way, but not when stopped.

Vessel fishing (other than trawling)

All-round red over white lights, plus sidelights and sternlight (if making way).When outlying gear extends more than 150 m an all-round white light (or, by day, a cone - point up) in the direction of the gear.

By day: trawlers and fishing vessels show a shape consisting of two cones with their points together.

Pilot vessel (Rule 29)

By day

SOUND SIGNALS

Vessels in sight of each other

One short blast
I am altering my
course to starboard.

Two short blasts
I am altering my
course to port.

Three short blasts
My engines are
running astern.

Five (or more) blasts
Your intentions
are not understood.
Keep clear.

Vessels in a narrow channel in sight of each other

**Two long & one
short blasts**
I intend to overtake you
on your starboard side.

**Two long & two
short blasts**
I intend to
overtake you
on your port side.

Morse Code 'C'
I agree to be
overtaken.

One long blast
I am approaching
a bend in the channel.

Note: one long blast, in reply, by an approaching vessel.

Vessels in restricted visibility

One long blast
every 2 minutes.
Power vessel underway.

Two long blasts
every 2 minutes.
Power vessel stopped.

One long & 2 short blasts
every 2 minutes.
Vessels under sail.
Also: vessels fishing,
towing, NUC, RAM, CBD.

Morse Code 'B' every
2 minutes. Vessel
under tow (if manned).

Vessels at Anchor

Rapid ringing of bell
for 5 seconds every minute.

**Vessel over
100m at anchor**
Bell rung forward.
Then gong rung rapidly
aft for 5 seconds.

May sound morse Code 'R' ■ ▬▬ ■ to warn
approaching vessel.

Vessels aground

Three rings of bell   Anchor signal   Three rings of bell

JARGON-BUSTER

Autohelm	A device for steering automatically
Backstay	An adjustable wire that pulls the mast aft (and bends it)
Bearing	Orientation in degrees from north
Beating	Zig-zagging towards the wind
Boom	Metal tube lying along the bottom of the mainsail
Bow	The forward part of the yacht
Bow roller	Roller over which the anchor and chain are raised and lowered
Call sign	Unique identifier used on the VHF radio e.g. C2JJ8
Chartplotter	Magic box (like a satnav) showing the boat's position and course on a digital chart
Cleat	A projecting fitting for attaching a rope temporarily
Clew	The lower, aft corner of a sail
Coachroof	The roof of the saloon
Companionway	The opening leading to the saloon
Cross track error	On a chartplotter: the distance the yacht is from the intended route
Dan buoy	A small floating buoy with a flag thrown overboard to mark the position of a Man Overboard
Decompressor	A flap in the top of a diesel engine. When open, the engine stops
Double	Loop a rope from yacht, around mooring cleat and back to yacht
Downhaul	A rope pulling downwards. The pole downhaul pulls the spinnaker pole downwards
DSC	Digital Selective Calling: the controller, which is a bit like a pager, sends a pulse with your details
Flake out	Lay out rope or chain in elongated S shapes to prevent tangling
Fo'c's'le	The forecabin
Foot	The bottom edge of a sail
Forestay	A fixed wire that pulls the mast forward
Galley	The boat's kitchen

Genoa	A headsail that overlaps the mast
Goosewinged	Running downwind with the genoa on the opposite side to the mainsail
Grabrail	A rail on deck or down below to grab hold of
Guardrails	Horizontal wires to keep the crew on board
Gybe	A turn where the stern of the boat crosses the wind
Gennaker	A downwind sail which is a cross between a large genoa and a spinnaker
GPS	The Global Positioning System, based on satellites' signals, gives your latitude and longitude anywhere in the world
Halyard	A rope or wire that hoists a sail
Head	The top corner of a sail
Heads	The toilet or toilet compartment
Head-to-wind	The boat aligned with the bows pointing into the wind and the sails flapping
Hove-to	Stopped, with the genoa aback and balancing the mainsail
Jackstay	Wires or lengths of webbing along each side deck. The crew clip on to these to move about the deck safely
Jammer	Deck hardware used to hold a rope under load
Kedge	A small secondary anchor
Kicking strap	Pulley system to pull down on the boom, also called the vang
Latitude	A measurement (in degrees) north or south of the equator. Shown on the vertical scale at the edge of a chart
Leech	The aft (vertical) edge of a sail
Leecloth	A canvas sheet hung to make a 'wall' to keep a sleeper in his bunk
Leeward	The side away from the wind
Liferaft	An inflatable boat with a canopy, launched when a yacht is in danger of sinking
Longitude	A measurement (in degrees) east or west of the Greenwich meridian. Shown on the horizontal scale at the edge of a chart

Lubber line	The vertical line in front of the compass against which the yacht's heading is read
Luff	The leading edge of a sail
Luff	To turn towards the wind
Mainsail	The sail set on the mast and boom, behind the genoa
Mainsheet	The rope that controls how far the boom, and therefore mainsail, is pulled in
Mayday	Raising the alarm when there is grave and imminent danger to a vessel or person
MOB	Man Overboard
No go area	An arc 45 degrees either side of the wind in which a yacht cannot sail because the sails just flap
Outhaul	A rope or wire that pulls the foot of the mainsail towards the aft end of the boom
Passerelle	A plank used for getting off the stern of a yacht onto the shore
Port	Left
Preventer	A rope system for holding the boom out when the yacht is running (preventing a gybe when the yacht rolls)
Pulpit	The stainless steel structure at the bow
Pushpit	The stainless steel structure at the stern
Range	Distance from the yacht to her destination
Reaching	Sailing at right angles to the wind
Reefing	Reducing sail area
Rhumb line	The straight line to the destination
Runners	Adjustable lines from the mast to the corners of the stern. When the windward one is tensioned it pulls the mast back, straightens the mast and straightens the luff of the genoa.
Running	Sailing away from the wind
Sail-tie	A piece of webbing tied around a sail after it has been lowered
Saloon	The living area of a yacht
Seacock	A valve in a pipe, next to the hull

Shackle	A metal hoop and pin used to attach one object to another
Shroud	A wire that supports the mast sideways
Spinnaker	A large downwind sail
Spreader	Horizontal arm projecting from the mast to give a shroud more leverage
Spring	A mooring rope that stops the boat moving forwards or backwards
Starboard	Right
Stanchion	A vertical rod that supports the lifelines
Stern	The aft part of the boat
Tack	A turn where the bow of the boat turns through the wind
Tack	The lower, forward corner of a sail
Take a turn	loop a rope once around
Telltale	A streamer on a sail to show the flow of air
Topping lift	A rope running from the end of the boom via the top of the mast and down to a cleat, used to lift the boom
Traveller	A slider on a track used to move the bottom of the mainsheet to windward or leeward
Toerail	A raised rail around the edge of the boat, where the hull meets the deck
Uphaul	A rope pulling upwards. The pole uphaul pulls up the spinnaker pole
Vang	A pulley system to pull down on the boom. Also called the kicking strap
Waypoint	A cross on an electronic chart, marking the boat's final or intermediate destination
Winch	A mechanical device to help wind in a rope, using a winch handle
Windex	A pivoted arrow at the top of the mast indicating the wind direction
Windlass	A machine for winding up the anchor chain
Windward	The side towards the wind